# Hitler Talk

Colin A. Thomson
William E. Lingard

*Hitler Talk* ©2009 Colin Thomson & William Lingard

Library and Archives Canada Cataloguing in Publication

Hitler talk / [edited by] Colin Thomson & William Lingard.

Includes bibliographical references.
ISBN 978-1-55059-365-5

1. Hitler, Adolf, 1889-1945-- Quotations.
I. Hitler, Adolf, 1889-1945
II. Thomson, Colin, 1938-
III. Lingard, William Eric, 1939-

DD247.H5H565 2009
943.086092
C2009-901561-7

All rights reserved. No part of this book can be reproduced in any form or by any means without written permission from the publisher.

We recognize the support of the government of Canada through the Book Publishing Industry Development Program (BPIDP) for our publishing program.

We also acknowledge the support of the Alberta Foundation for the Arts for our publishing program.

SAN 113-0234
ISBN 978-1-55059-365-5
Printed in Canada
Cover design by James Dangerous

DETSELIG
ENTERPRISES LTD

210 · 1220 Kensington Rd NW
Calgary, Alberta T2N 3P5
www.temerondetselig.com

p. 403-283-0900
f. 403-283-6947
e. temeron@telusplanet.net

# Acknowledgements

The production of this book has required assistance from several people.

Irma Dogterom worked many hours copying the original draft and then making numerous changes and revisions, always with a smile and a positive comment.

We would also like to thank Kimberley Finn for her assistance with pictures.

Finally to our editor, James Dangerous, goes our appreciation for his help and guidance in the preparation of this book.

*The real search for Hitler – the search for who he was, who he thought he was, and why he did what he did is what he hid within him. It's a trek into the trackless realm of Hitler's inwardness. A terra cotta incognita of ambiguity and incertitude where armies of scholars clash in evidentiary darkness over the spectral shadows of Hitler's past and the maddening obscurities of his psyche.*

Ron Rosenbaum

# Table of Contents

Introduction 11

Childhood: 1889 - 1905 15
Young Manhood: 1905-1914 25
The Soldier: 1914-1918 35
Rise of the Nazi Party: 1919-1923 47
Prison & the Lean Years 1924-1932 59
Triumph: 1933-1936 69
Power & Appeasement: 1937-1939 77
The Man 85
Racism 107
Anti Semitism 111
Education, Propaganda, & Symbolism 123
Hitler & Women 139
Leadership & The Big Lies 151
The Politician 173
Religion 181
North American Response 185
After Words 193

Sequence of Events 219
Appendix 235
Bibliography 253

*To Juanita and Eleanor, for their patience and encouragement during this project.*

# Introduction

The evil genius Adolf Hitler, the greatest criminal of all time, the most powerful ruler of the modern era, the greatest mover and shaker of the 20th Century, master of the big lie, dictator, madman, mass murderer, military bungler, arbiter of the fate of world peace and the lives of millions, the creator of Nazism, courageous and decorated German corporal, was born at 6:30 p.m. on April 20, 1889, in the small town of Braunau on the River Inn, which formed the frontier between Bavaria and Austria.

*Mussolini was born in 1883. Stalin was born in 1879. Lenin was born in 1870.*

Both Hitler's voice (he was a persuasive and powerful orator – rabble rouser – propagandist) and his written words clearly told the world what he intended to do. For too long, his listeners and readers ignored his threats and hateful commentary. Perhaps as many as fifty million people lost their lives during the 1939-1945 war: a result of Hitlerism, hate, barbarism and apathy. It seems likely that we will never fully understand the terrible experiences which befell the world during the twelve years of Hitler's Third Reich.

The world must remember that on Hitler's order, millions of innocent people were maimed, tortured, and murdered.

However, some semblance of clarity can be had by "listening" to Adolf Hitler's comments, and by considering the response to these statements.

If the price of liberty is eternal vigilance, then today we must listen to other voices resonant of Hitler and act accordingly. Therefore, it seems wise that we read and reread the lies and other observations of that raspy-voiced, staring-eyed, toothbrush-mustached, narrow-shouldered, spindly-legged, wide-hipped, cowlick-graced, paranoiac vandal, Adolf Hitler.

*Hitler's book Mein Kampf (My Struggle) is often considered a Satanic bible.*

His April 30, 1945 suicide did not end his impact, even though it concluded a most intriguing and puzzling career, that of a megalomaniac who believed sincerely that providence had chosen him to be his nation's savior.

Serious readers know that there are many excellent biographies of Hitler. His youth, rise to power, political successes, World War II victories and defeats, and his last days have been recorded by camera and print. This book is not intended to be a history of Nazism or a biography of the ruthless dictator. The book's sole intent is to inform and remind today's readers that Hitler's statements, and those about him, can inspire those readers to learn more about that enigmatic, political genius, the Chaplinesque man-turned-monster with a Messiah complex.

To ignore that past is to live dangerously.

How could that Bavarian ex-corporal, an unprepossessing specimen, even with such a dominating personality (a basis for his appeal) and with such a sadistic craving for power sway and take charge of the majority of some sixty million people living in a most literate and culture-rich nation? How could a nation that gave us Schiller, Schuman, Goethe, and Beethoven also produce an Auschwitz, a Belsen, a Dachau, and other horrors?

Some of these answers are found in Hitler's own words, and in reactions to them.

By the time World War II began, Hitler's aims, personality and evil had been clearly formed. Therefore, this book dealing with the tyrant stops at that date.

From the Atlantic to the Caucasus, and from the Arctic to the Sahara, the power of Adolf Hitler was cruelly in evidence. He conquered twenty-two countries, left much of Europe in rubble, and caused the death of millions of people. If only his voice had been heard by other leaders or taken seriously... READ ON!

*Readers will note that some sources spell Hitler's first name "Adolph." Fuhrer is also spelt "Fuehrer."*

# Chapter 1
## Childhood: 1889 – 1905

*Children are hopes.*
Novalis

*The childhood shows the man
as morning shows the day.*
John Milton

## Hitler Quotes

My father was a [dutiful] civil servant, my mother giving all her being to her household ... [and] to us children.

I had honored my father, but my mother I had loved.

I then resolved never again to cry when my father whipped me.

Klara and Alois Hitler, mother and father of Adolf.

I would never be happy as a civil servant...

Fate itself became my instructor...

At the Realschule I had been by far the best in my class at drawing... [and] my talent for painting seemed to be excelled by my talent for drawing...

I was still so busy with my own destiny that I could not concern myself with the people around me.

As a boy I was no pacifist, and all attempts to educate me in this direction came to nothing.

# Comments and Reaction

Both Hitler and Jesus of Nazareth were born in an inn. Bizarre though the conjunction may seem, it would not have displeased the Führer, in spite of his rancid contempt for the Christian faith.

*Ronald Lewin*

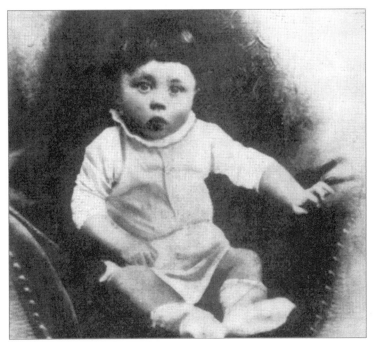

The infant Hitler

Hitler's early life . . . was not one of hardship and poverty. Contrary to the impression he conveys in *Mein Kampf*, he was neither poor nor harshly treated. -Bullock

The boy [Hitler] was bright enough at school although he already showed signs of being both self-willed and resistant to the discipline of regular work. -Bullock

> Hitler's marks for the first semester at the Realschule in Steyr were:
>
> | | | |
> |---:|:---:|:---|
> | Moral conduct | 3 | satisfactory |
> | Diligence | 4 | erratic |
> | Religion | 4 | adequate |
> | Geography & history | 4 | adequate |
> | Mathematics | 5 | satisfactory |
> | Chemistry | 4 | adequate |
> | Physics | 3 | satisfactory |
> | Geometry | 4 | adequate |
> | Freehand drawing | 2 | praiseworthy |
> | Gymnastics | 1 | excellent |
> | Stenography | 5 | inadequate |
> | Handwriting | 5 | unpleasing |
>
> *-Payne*

From *Mein Kampf* about his early years where he was always at the top of his class – He speaks of the "flowering" of his ideals. "Much romping in the open air, the long walk to school and the companionship of unusually robust boys, caused my mother grievous suffering but this did not prevent me from becoming the opposite of a stay-at-home. I believe that even then my talent for making speeches was being developed in the more or less violent arguments with my school fellows. I had become a ringleader and at school learned easily and well but I was otherwise rather difficult to handle.

[Hitler] challenged his father to extreme harshness and got his sound thrashing every day. He was a scrubby little rogue . . . -Payne

There is a slight possibility that Hitler's grandfather was a wealthy Jew named Frankenberger or Franemeither. -Toland

*Most experts claim that there is no proof to support this view of Hitler's lineage.*

In play he was inspired by the adventure stories . . . by James Fenimore Cooper. -Toland

He was a quiet fanatic [as a boy] . . . -Toland

His schoolmaster remembered Adolf as mentally very much alert, obedient, but lively. -Toland

Adolf was a Mother's Boy (*Mutter sunnchen*) devoted to his mother all his life he kept a photo of his mother with him – He kept no photo of his father – He seldom spoke of him and then with suppressed fury. By being so devoted to his mother he ensured that he would find no women equal to her . . . -Payne

Adolf "lived only for his mother." -Toland

To Klara, Adolf's mother, "he was a young prince with slumbering talent, obviously destined for fame." -Toland

As a small boy it was his most ardent wish to become a priest. He often borrowed the large kitchen apron of the maid, draped it about his shoulders in vestment fashion . . . and delivered long and fervent sermons. -Toland

Hitler's father tried to force that career upon him. Initially the youth wanted to become a painter. That work brought him very modest success. -Kjelle

I well remember a gaunt pale-faced boy. He was gifted in a one-sided way for he lacked self-control and to say the least was regarded as argumentative, willful, arrogant and bad tempered, and notoriously incapable of submitting to school discipline. He was not industrious. If he was we would have achieved better results with his undoubted ability. *-Prof. Eduard Humer, Linz Realschule*

He reacted with hostility when reproved or given advice by a teacher, at the same time demanding unqualified subservience of his fellow pupils, fancying himself in the role of leader. *-Payne*

Hitler (Top Center) with classmates.

Father and son quarreled bitterly and often. Alois [the father] called Adolf lazy and daffy, and [was] probably right on both counts, but Adolf grew up hating "book learning." By the time he was fifteen,

Adolf had attended five different secondary schools. -*Gervais*

Adolf's teachers did not have a high opinion of him ... He was notoriously cantankerous, willful, arrogant, and bad tempered. -*Gervais*

[Adolf, the boy] looks sickly, with a round smallish head, and a soft milky white face, but with the staring eyes and unmistakable cowlick of the Führer he became. -*Gervais*

Adolph spent more time shooting rats, reading and drawing than on school work. -*Toland*

He wandered the streets of Linz, solitary but not lonesome – his mind churning with dreams of the future. -*Toland*

The most striking thing about Hitler's childhood is that it lasted until his death. He had no capacity for intellectual, emotional, artistic, or sexual development. -*Waite*

[In 1904 at his confirmation at church] "none was so sulky and surly as Adolph Hitler. I had to drag the words out of him," according to his sponsor. -*Toland*

Young Adolf was a willful, indulgent child with strong opinions. His early education was satisfactory, but he was a total failure in the secondary, technical school in the city of Linz. -Kjelle

One of his teachers remembered Hitler as a "lively, bright eyed, and intelligent six-year-old who came to school hand-in-hand with his twelve-year-old sister Angela [and] both children were neat and orderly." -Gervais

*Cf. Payne*

[As a boy,] Adolf was sometimes seen at night sitting on the cemetery wall, gazing up at the stars. -Payne

Loneliness, too, played an important part in the sudden change that came over him, [and] the boy found solace in a dream world, sank deeper and deeper into himself. -Payne

One of Hitler's teachers reported that Hitler "used to hold conversations with the windblown trees." -Payne

[Hitler was a] scrawny, scraggly youth, pale and intense . . . with a poor record of scholarship and his laziness. -Payne

As a child Hitler must have felt his lack very keenly for throughout his later life we find him searching for a strong masculine figure whom he can respect and emulate. *-Langer*

# Chapter 2
## Young Manhood: 1905 - 1914

*For the imagination of man's heart
is evil from his youth.*
Genesis 8:21

*Nobody can be so amusingly arrogant as
a young man who has just discovered an old idea
and thinks it is his own.*
Sydney Harris

## Hitler Quotes

With a suitcase full of clothes and underwear in my hand and an indomitable will in my heart, I set out for Vienna . . . I too hoped to become "something."

I did not have to learn much [by age nineteen] to add to what I created for myself.

[That time in Vienna was] the saddest period of my life. *1909-1913*

[By my 20th year] fate itself became my instructor.

I had to get out into the great Reich [from Austria] to Munich the land of my dreams and my longing.

In the years 1909 and 1910, my own situation had changed . . . [and] I painted to make a living and studied for pleasure [and] . . . was firmly convinced that I should some day make a name for myself as an architect.

With the passing years I became more and more interested in architecture.

At the age of seventeen the word "Marxism" was as yet little known to me . . . Here again it required the fist of Fate to open my eyes to this unprecedented betrayal of the peoples.

This teacher [Dr. Leopold Potasch] made history my favorite subject.

Thus at an early age, I had become a political "revolutionary," and I became an artistic revolutionary.

[After moving to Vienna there were] five years in which I was forced to earn a living, first as a day laborer, then as a small painter, a truly meager living which never sufficed to appease my daily hunger. Hunger was then my faithful bodyguard ... My life was a continuous struggle with this pitiless friend.

When thus for the first time I recognized the Jew as the cold-hearted, shameless, and calculating director of this revolting vice traffic is the scum of the big city, a cold shudder ran down my back.

I had at last come to the conclusion that the Jew was no German.

Inspired by the experience of daily life, I now began to track down the [Jewish] source of the Marxist doctrine ... the Jewish doctrine of Marxism rejects the aristocratic principle of Nature.

Hitler claimed that in his youth he learned two main things: "I became a nationalist [pan-Germanism] and I learned to understand and grasp the meaning of history."

Hardly had the news of the assassination become known "... two thoughts quivered through my brain: first that at last war would be inevitable; and ... the Hapsburg state would be compelled to keep its pact." *The murder of Archduke Ferdinand of Austria, June 28, 1914*

As a boy and young man I had so often felt the desire to prove . . . by deeds that for me national enthusiasm was no empty whim.

I had ceased to be a weak-kneed cosmopolitan and became an anti-Semitic.

[Hitler recalled] "the [youthful] nightmare vision of the seduction of hundreds of thousands of girls by repulsive, crooked-legged Jew bastards."

When not yet twenty years old, I set foot . . . in the House of Deputies as a spectator and listener, I was seized with the most conflicting sentiments . . . [and] soon was I to grow indignant when I saw the lamentable comedy that unfolded beneath my eyes . . . I couldn't help laughing.

## Comments and Reaction

When at the age of fourteen the young man is discharged from school, it is hard to decide what is stronger in him: his incredible stupidity . . . or the corrosive insolence of his behavior . . . which would make your hair stand on end. -*Payne*

Klara died, and her doctor said of son Adolf: "I never saw anyone so prostrate with grief."
-Payne

[Hitler] was a failed artist with a Bohemian lifestyle who possessed one great gift: the ability to move crowds with his rhetoric. -Evans

Whatever the reason, for the next five years he chose to bury himself in obscurity. -Bevin

*1908-1913*

At the Vienna opera house, Hitler would not sit in the gallery with girls because "all they were after was flirting." -Toland

After failing to gain entry to an art academy, Hitler asked; "Or has fate chosen me for something else?"
- Toland

August Kubizek recalled Hitler as a youth who saw everywhere obstacles and hostility [and] was always at odds with the world [and] avoided any relations with women. -Gervais

Hitler's friend August Kubizek.

Kubizek considered Hitler to be exceedingly violent and high-strung. -*Toland*

[Reinhold Hanisch, a fellow painter from Vienna] said that "next to me sat a man with nothing on but an old torn pair of trousers – Adolf Hitler. His clothes were being deloused." -*Gervais*

In Munich, Adolph resumed the friendless, penniless, vagabond existence that had become his way of life. -*Gervais*

And in Munich, as in Vienna, Hitler avoided all contact with women. -*Gervais*

Hitler lived a solitary life. He had no other friends [except Kubizek]. Women were attracted to him, but he showed complete indifference to them. Much of the time he spent dreaming or brooding. -*Bevin*

The young Hitler was impatient, moody, irritable if contradicted, and prone to outbursts of temper. -*Kjelle*

He neither smoked nor drank [and] was too shy and awkward to have any success with women. His passions were reading newspapers and talking politics . . . he became more eccentric, more turned in on himself. He struck people as unbalanced. *-Bevin*

[In Vienna] wherever he looked he saw injustice, hate and enmity. *-Toland*

In Vienna "he wandered for the next three months, a tramp. He slept in parks and doorways. ... Even now I [Hitler] think of those pitiful dens ... those sinister pictures of dirt and repugnant filth and worse still." *-Toland*

The anti-Semitic politician Karl Lueger spoke of young Hitler's involvement in political discussions: "When he got excited Hitler couldn't restrain himself. He screamed and fidgeted with his hands." *-Toland*

The political prejudices of his adolescence became the political program of the German dictator. *-Waite*

[Young Hitler] became something of a dandy, affecting black kid gloves, a derby hat, and an ivory-handled mahogany walking stick. *-Waite*

There is no evidence that he ever painted a house, hung wallpaper, or worked as a manual laborer. *-Waite*

Hitler was . . . the sum of his own inner compulsions to power which stemmed from deeply rooted psychological problems traceable to the circumstances of his birth, childhood and upbringing. -Gervais

At nineteen he already thought he knew everything that was to be known. -Gervais

The years in Vienna, from 1909 to 1913, were the hardest and unhappiest in Hitler's life. -Jarman

*Hitler kept that opinion for the rest of his life.*

There was a period, between sixteen and eighteen, when Hitler's image of himself began to take shape . . . it was the image of a heroic rebel . . . and that of an artistic genius. -Bullock

Hitler's Vienna friend Kubizek said Adolf was "completely out of balance." -Bullock

The turn of the year 1909-10 saw him touching his lowest point: hungry, homeless, without an overcoat, physically weak and with no idea what to do . . . his troubles were of his own making. -Bullock

In Bavarian leather breeches, short thick woolen socks, a red-blue-checked shirt and a short blue jacket that bagged about his unpadded skeleton, his sharp cheekbones stuck out over hollow, pasty cheeks, and above them was a pair of unnaturally bright-blue eyes, there was a half-starved look about him, but something else too, a sort of fanatical look. -*Description of young Hitler by Friedelind, Composer Wagner's granddaughter.*

As a young man he had no control over his imagination, possessed almost no critical ability, and seemed to take pains to be erratic. -*Payne*

Something obscure happened in his mind at the onset of adolescence, and he developed an obscene hatred of the stronger male. -*Wells*

Hitler at the proclamation of World War I.

Through the dingy years before the war (WWI), this unstable creature had gone about dreaming and muttering to himself; he seems never to have earned a living by his industry, and to have sunk to rags and the common doss-house . . . -*Wells*

When war broke out in 1914, it was for Hitler a tremendous release, a chance to identify with German Nationalism at last. -*Stone*

# Chapter 3
## The Soldier
## 1914 - 1918

*Soldiers are citizens of death's grey land.*
Siegfried Sassoon, 1918

*War is the science of destruction.*
John S.C. Abbott

## Hitler Quotes

[After the first Battle of Ypres] there were only thirty officers left in the whole regiment. Four companies had to be dissolved. But we were all proud of having licked the Britishers.

*Hitler makes it sound like a German victory.*
*- Gervais*

In a badly worded letter from the front to his ex-landlord, Hitler stated: We want an all-out fight at any cost, and we hope that those of us who have the good fortune to see their homeland again will find it purer and more purified of foreignism; that through the sacrifices and sufferings which hundreds of us go through every day, that through an international world of enemies, not only Germany's enemies will be crushed, but that our internal internationalism will also be broken. That would be worth more than any territorial gains. With Austria it will come as I have always said ... While the list of those proposed [for decorations] was being compiled four company commanders came into our tent. Due to lack of space, the four of us soldiers had to step out. We hadn't been outside five minutes when an enemy grenade struck the tent, gravely wounded Lieutenant Colonel Engelhardt and killed the others. It was the most terrible moment of my life.

*The event convinced Hitler that he was under Divine protection and guidance.*

The struggle of the year 1914 was not forced on the masses – no, by the living God – it was desired by the people.

*The beginning of the 1914-1918 Great War.*

Overpowered by stormy enthusiasm I fell down on my knees and thanked Heaven from an overflowing heart for granting me the good fortune of being permitted to live at this time.

My own position on the conflict was ... that Germany was fighting for her existence, the German nation for life or death, freedom and future.

The aim for which we were fighting the War was the loftiest, the most overpowering, that men can conceive ... the German nation was engaged in a struggle for existence.

My heart ... overflowed with proud joy that at last I would be able to redeem myself.

*At the war's outbreak*

[When permission arrived which allowed my acceptance into a Bavarian Regiment] my joy and gratitude knew no bounds. A few days later I was wearing the tunic which I was not to doff until nearly six years later.

For me ... there now began the greatest and most unforgettable time of my earthly existence ...

In October, 1914, we ... burned with stormy enthusiasm as we crossed the border.

[On the train to the front] I felt as though my heart would burst.

In October and November of 1914 we received there our baptism of fire. Fatherland love in our heart and songs on our lips, our young regiments [went] into the battle as to a dance. The most precious blood there sacrificed itself joyfully.

And then came a damp, cold night in Flanders, through which we marched in silence, and when the day began to emerge from the mists, suddenly an iron greeting came whizzing at us over our heads, and with a sharp report sent the little pellets flying between our ranks, ripping up the wet ground; but even before the little cloud had passed, from two hundred throats the first hurrah rose to meet the first messenger of death. Then a crackling and a roaring, a singing and a howling began, and with feverish eyes each one of us was drawn forward, faster and faster, until suddenly past turnip fields and hedges the fight of man against man. And from the distance the strains of a song reached our ears, coming closer and closer, leaping from company to company, and just as Death plunged a busy hand into our ranks, the song reached us too and we passed it along: *Deutschland, Deutschland über Alles, übre Alles in der Welt!*

-Hitler, *Mein Kampf*

By the winter of 1915-16 . . . my will was undisputed master . . . Now fate could bring on the ultimate tests without my nerves shattering or my reason failing. The young volunteer had become an old soldier.

I was a soldier then and I didn't want to talk politics.

The volunteers of [my] List Regiment . . . knew how to die like old soldiers.

If the best men were dying at the front, the least we could do was to wipe out the [Jewish] vermin.

At the end of September, 1916, my division moved into the Battle of the Somme, [and] it was more like hell than war.

With the year 1915 enemy propaganda began in our country [and], at the beginning of 1918 it swelled to a positive flood.

I felt for the first time the whole malice of Destiny which kept me . . . where every nigger might shoot me to bits . . . But I was a nameless soldier, me among eight million!

On October 7, 1916, I was wounded. I was brought safely to the rear . . . Two years had now passed since I had seen my homeland . . . the Fatherland.

During the nights [while in hospital] my hatred increased – hatred for the originators of this dastardly crime. There was no such thing as coming to an understanding with the Jews. It must be the hard-and-fast "Either-Or."

[As a patient] for the first time I heard . . . men bragging about their own cowardice . . . Disgust mounted in my throat.

While [soldiers] starved and suffered, while their people lived at home in misery, there was abundance and high-living in other circles.

At the beginning of March, 1917, I was back with my regiment.

*By the Treaty of Brest-Litovsk, the Russians were to turn over huge areas, i.e. Ukraine, to Germany.*

[In 1917] the whole army took fresh hope and fresh courage after the Russian collapse.

In July 1917, we set foot for the second time on the ground that was sacred to all of us. For in it slumbered [those] who had run to their deaths with gleaming eyes for one true Fatherland.

I had the good fortune to fight in the first two offensives.

Now, in the fall of 1918, we stood for the third time on the storm site of 1914 ... Now in a hand-defensive battle the regiment was to defend the soil which it had stormed three years earlier.

On the night of October 13 the English gas attack [took place] ... I, too, was seized with pain which grew worse with every quarter hour, and at seven in the morning I stumbled and tottered back with burning eyes ... [and] a few hours later my eyes had turned into glowing coals; it had grown dark around me.

[Later] I [was] getting better, the piercing pain in my eye sockets was diminishing slowly.

[After learning of the German defeat] everything went black before my eyes; I tottered and groped my way back to the dormitory, threw myself on my bunk, and dug my head into my blanket and pillow ... And so it had all been in vain.

> *Another source gave a similar description: "Lance Corporal Hitler ... threw himself sobbing on to his hospital bed in Pasewalk and, wiping tears of rage, swore to become a politician."*
> *-Hoffman*

# Comments and Reaction

The fact that Austria, his homeland, would inevitably be destroyed gave him intense pleasure. It was as though the war had come about only in order to avenge his own private sufferings in Austria. -Payne

Unknown to him at the time, there were two men in the Regiment whom he would influence profoundly in years to come. One was Max Amann ... the other man was Rudolf Hess. -Payne

As a twenty-five-year-old volunteer, Hitler was surrounded by recruits much younger than himself. He was reserved, rather diffident, incapable of small talk. In later years he spoke as if he had "shared the common joys and griefs of the soldiers," but this was not the impression he made on them. There was something uncomfortably wayward about him; he did not quite fit in with the others and held himself a little apart. -Payne

Ignaz Westenkirchner, Dispatch Runner and close friend, remembered Hitler as a man who seemed unusually serious and almost pedantic. Everything had to be done according to the rules. -Payne

Another soldier called Hitler "a peculiar fellow."
... He sat in a corner, with his helmet on his head, buried deep in thought, and none of us was able to rouse him from his listlessness . . . He received no letters, no parcels from home. He did not care about leave or women. -*Bullock*

We all cursed him. We found him intolerable. He was a white crow among us who wouldn't go along with us when we damned the war to hell and prayed for its speedy end. -*Army Comrade of Hitler*

Hitler was rescued from his existence as a bohemian on the margins of cultural life by the outbreak of the First World War. -*Evans*

Hitler was developing a critical attitude toward the German High Command and sometimes found himself wondering whether they possessed the will power and determination to succeed. -*Payne*

Hitler led a charmed life during the war. -*Payne*

What sort of a soldier was Hitler? As early as December 1914, he had been awarded the Iron Cross, Second Class [and] the Iron Cross, First Class, in 1918. -*Bullock*

*It was unusual for a "common soldier" to receive the First Class honor.*

Corporal Hitler

The few photographs of this time [late 1918] show a solemn pale face, prematurely old, with staring eyes. He took the war seriously, feeling personally responsible for what happened, and identifying himself with the failure in success in German arms. -*Bullock*

During his four years at the front Hitler never asked to leave, never received packages, and rarely received any letters. -*Comrade of Hitler*

The 1914-1918 war gave Hitler "for the first time in his life a cause, a commitment, comradeship, an external discipline . . . a sense of belonging." -*Kershaw*

Despite being described as an 'odd character' by one comrade in arms, Adolf was happy in his role as soldier. -*Toland*

The war and the impact of war upon the individual lives of millions of Germans, were among the essential conditions for the rise of Hitler and the Nazi Party. -*Bullock*

The war [1914-1918] which would bring death to millions of young men, brought for Adolf Hitler, at twenty-nine, a new start in life. -*Shirer*

"Suddenly," said a fellow soldier at the front, "he would leap up, run about excitedly, and shout that in spite of our big guns victory would be denied us, for the invisible foes of the German people were a greater danger than the biggest cannon of the enemy." -*Gervais*

Lt. Colonel Engelhardt praised Hitler as "an exceedingly brave, effective, and conscientious soldier." -*Gervais*

[After WWI] the downfall of Germany seemed to him inexplicable by ordinary processes. Somewhere there had been a gigantic and monstrous betrayal. Lonely and pent within himself, the little soldier pondered and speculated. -*Churchill*

For Pfc. Hitler, the List Regiment was his homeland. -*A fellow soldier.*

Hitler himself declared that the war had transformed him. It hardened this touchy and sentimental young man and gave him a sense of his own worth . . . but the war also magnified Hitler's tendency to brooding. -*Fest*

Having no family, no home address, no destination whatsoever, he had renounced his right to furloughs. His superzeal untroubled, he stayed on in his unreal world [on the battlefields]. -*Fest*

# Chapter 4
## Rise of the Nazi Party: 1919 - 1923

*Struggle is the father of all things.*
Adolf Hitler

*The Führer is the party
and the party is the Führer.*
Adolf Hitler

*The man [Hitler] is dangerous;
he believes what he says.*
Joseph Goebbels

## Hitler Quotes.

| | |
|---|---|
| When I was confined to bed the idea came to me that I would liberate Germany, that I would make it great. | *1918* |
| We need a dictator who is a genius. | *1920* |

After an early speech in Munich, Hitler said that "by it, [the speech] the party burst the narrow bonds of a small club, and for the first time exerted a determining influence on the mightiest factor [of] our time, public opinion.

"Down with the November criminals!" That must be our slogan.

1922 Our motto shall be - if you will not be a German, I will bash your skull in. For we are convinced that we cannot succeed without a struggle. We have to fight with ideas, but, if necessary, also with our fists.

Hitler leaving an early Nazi Party meeting.

The German spirit cannot be broken ... Germany [in 1923] is awakening, the German freedom movement is on the march.

I want now to fulfill a vow which I made to myself five years ago when I was a blind cripple in the military hospital: to know neither rest nor peace until the November criminals had been overthrown. *1923, failed Beer Hall Putsch*

As though by an explosion our ideas were hurled over the whole of Germany. *As a result of the failed Putsch*

Our revolution will never be complete until we have dehumanized human beings.

The national revolution has begun ... troops and police are marching on the city under the banner of the swastika. *Nov. 8, 1923*

If in the struggle I should fall, the swastika banner shall be my shroud.

On the day when Marxism is smashed in Germany, her fetters will in truth be broken forever.

On Feb. 24, 1920, Hitler spoke to two thousand people, and gave first reading of the twenty-five-point party program in *Mein Kampf*. *See Appendix A*

Hitler describes the scene: "The screaming and shouting were slowly drowned out by the applause".

*At first attendance at a German Workers Party meeting*

I spoke, the audience had listened with astonished faces.

I was facing the hardest question of my life: should I join or should I decline. So I registered as a member . . . and received a provisional membership with the number 7.

*Hitler leapt on to a table and fired at the ceiling to secure attention as he announced his intention to take over the government.*

As Nationalist Socialists we see our program in our flag. In the red we see the social idea of movement, in the white the national idea, in the swastika the mission to struggle for the victory of Aryan man and at the same time the victory of the idea of creative which is eternally anti-Semitic . . . "The National Revolution has begun."

I alone bear the responsibility [for the putsch] but . . . there is no such thing as high treason against the traitors of 1918.

At Hitler's 1924 trial [for treason] his closing comment was, "I believe that the hour will come when the masses, who today stand in the street with our swastika banner, will unite with those who fired upon them."

This is absolutely a new beginning. [Feb. 27, 1925] You must forget your personal quarrels. If you do not, I shall start the party alone, without you.

## Comments and Reaction

In the summer of 1921, as ruthless in his quest for power as he was indefatigable, he took over undisputed leadership of the Nazi party. -*Gervais*

After the armistice, Hitler returned to Munich, where he met racist agitators who confirmed his childhood beliefs. His hatred for Jews became intensified. -*Waite*

In November, 1923 he had thought himself within an inch of becoming dictator of Germany ... and now he was only the obscure leader of an illegal political party with perhaps a hundred loyal followers. -*Payne*

From the beginning of his political career Hitler had given himself three aims -- the political unification of the German people, the destruction of the Jews in Germany, and the uprooting of Bolshevism from the earth. -*Payne*

*Hitler was given the minimum sentence of five years imprisonment, but was released after serving less than nine months in Landsberg prison. Hitler and some 40 others had a rather comfortable and easy life there.*

In the midsummer of 1920 the new flag (Swastika) appeared in public for the first time. It was wonderfully suited for the young movement and it was as young and new as the movement.
No one had ever seen it before – it was like a blazing token. *-Payne*

In the Autumn of 1922 Hermann Goering, holder of Germany's highest decoration for bravery under fire, heard Hitler speak, and was attracted to the movement. Others followed. *-Bullock*

Hitler's Nazism was a phenomena which throve only in conditions of disorder and insecurity. *-Bullock*

A shot rang out and a hail of bullets swept the street and Hitler fell. He was either pulled down or was seeking cover. Sixteen Nazis and three police lay dead or dying in the street after the Beer Hall incident. *-Bullock*

Demagogy had restored him the identity he had lost with the German defeat. He had left the army and became a full-time political agitator. *-Evans*

In 1921 . . . Hitler was at the centre of another beer-cellar brawl [in Munich] with beer mugs flying across the room as Nazis and Social

Democrats traded blows. Some of the Nazis were arming themselves with knuckle-dusters, rubber truncheons, pistols, and even grenades. -Evans

His party, founded in 1919, was more dynamic, more ruthless, and more violent than other extreme-right-wing fringe groups. -Evans

This small party of mediocrities [the German Workers' Party] gave Hitler . . . an opportunity to play a leading role. -Kjelle

*Hitler's party number was fifty-five, and executive member number was seven.*

Early Nazi Party meeting.

*See Appendix A*  At the beginning Hitler had made it clear that the path to power lay through aggression and violence against a Weimar Republic born from the shame of defeat. -Churchill

Hitler's [early] speeches put him on the political map in Munich but he was still very much a local. -Kershaw

Street orator, Munich 1923.

Without the individual magnetism of Hitler there would have been no Nazi Party -*Darmon*

Here he found a calling as a rabble-rousing political speaker – when Hitler investigated in 1919 the German Workers' Party, an anti-Semitic and nationalist group. -*Crew*

Hitler emerged in the post-war years as the fanatical champion of German nationalism. -*Jarman*

Yet so far Hitler had given few signs of greatness. -*Jarman*  1921

[A follower of Hitler said of the man's speech] . . . glancing round, I saw his magnetism was holding these thousands as me. -*Jarman*  1922

Hitler's *Mein Kampf* . . . is remarkable because it set out ideas and obstacles . . . Hitler was able to carry out in practice. -*Jarman*

"I have the impression he's [Hitler] going to play a big part, and whether you like him or not, he certainly knows what he wants." -*American ambassador Truman Smith*  1922

"The final solution." A euphemistic term of Hitler's referring to the extermination of Europe's Jews.

By 1923 Hitler and the Nazi Party felt no particular need to look respectable. Violence seemed the obvious way to power. -Evans

*Historian Karl Alexander von Muller heard Hitler speak in 1923, and noted Hitler's "inner fanaticism"*

"His eyes glanced from right to left as if looking for enemies to conquer. [It was] fanatically hysteric romanticism with a brutal will." -von Muller

As one observer noted in 1923, "Hitler now had definite Napoleonic and Messianic ideas. He declared that he felt the call within himself to save Germany and that this role would fall to him." -Toland

Hitler changed the name of the party to National Socialist German Workers' Party (Nationalsozialistische Deutsche Arbeiterparti) which was abbreviated to NSDAP or Nazi Party for the first two syllables. -Waite

*1924* Hitler entered prison convinced his own destiny had turned on him but now through rationalization he had persuaded himself that it had saved him. -Toland

It was remarkable how Hitler had gained ascendancy over his jailors [at Landsberg Prison]. He had already converted a majority of the staff to National Socialism -Toland

Throughout the summer Hitler luxuriated in his pleasant quarters, preparing himself for the battle to come. -Toland

*In prison*

It grows more and more clear that his purpose is simply to use the Nationalist Socialist party as a springboard for his own immoral purposes, and to seize leadership in order to force the party onto a different track . . . This is most clearly shown by an ultimatum which he sent to the party leaders a few days ago, in which he demands, among other things, that he shall have a sole and absolute dictatorship of the party, and that the committee, including . . . Anton Drexler, founder and the leader of the party, should retire -*Gervais*

*Drexler was made an honorary president, but Hitler was named president. The humiliated Drexler left the party in 1923.*

# Chapter 5
## Prison and the Lean Years: 1924 - 1932

*The vilest deeds like poison weeds,*
*Bloom well in prison air.*
Oscar Wilde

*Tyrants have always some slight shade of virtue:*
*They support the laws before destroying them.*
Voltaire 1691-1778

## Hitler Quotes - Prison

If the German nation today, penned into an impossible area, faces a lamentable future, this is not a commandment of Fate.   *1924*

*According to the prison psychologist, Hitler stated:*
"I've had enough. I'm finished. If I had a revolver, I would take it."

*Hitler speaking at his trial for treason, a 24-day event beginning Feb 26, 1924. He and eight others were found guilty.*

If today I stand here as a revolutionary, it is a revolutionary against the revolution. There is no such thing as high treason against the traitors of 1918.

The goddess of the eternal court of history will smile and tear to tatters the brief of the state prosecutor and the sentence of this court. For she acquits us.

The judges of this state may go right ahead and convict us ... but History ... will one day smilingly tear up this verdict, acquitting us of all guilt and blame.

*While in prison, to Hess*

I shall need five years before the movement is on top again.

## Comments and Reaction

It was the trial that was the making of the Nazis. Hitler dominated the trial with his personality and speaking, and emerged as an international figure
-Collins

The failure of the Putsch had made Hitler realize that ... he would have to use it (democracy) to come to the position of power from which he could destroy it. -*Collins*

Hitler went to prison ... and wrote *Mein Kampf*, a confused, illiterate, schoolboy production, a book as common as the swill of beer wiped from a cafe table. -*Wells*

For every word in *Mein Kampf* 125 lives were lost, for every page, 4,700 lives, for every chapter, more than 1,200,000 lives. -*Gervais*

For all its author's guile and treachery, *Mein Kampf* was never deliberately vague. -*Darmon*

If [other leaders] had read it with the attention it deserves, they would have seen what was a blueprint for the ... conquest of the world. -*Payne*

No one can say that Adolf Hitler did not give full warning of the barbarian world he intended to make it. -*Shirer*

Except for the Bible, Hitler's book *Mein Kampf* was the "best seller" during the Nazi regime. By the time WWII began, six million copies had been sold in Germany. Between eight and nine million copies of *Mein Kampf* were sold during Hitler's lifetime, making him rich.

## Hitler Quotes - Lean Years

The SA is not a moral institution for the education of well-to-do daughters, but an association of rough fighters.

1932 Once we have power, we will never surrender it unless we are carried out of our offices as corpses.

We shall have to hold our noses and enter the Reichstag.

Hitler in Landsberg Prison

*Hitler used Hindenburg to gain power:*

> I need that feeble-minded old bull. Say what you will, his prestige is still priceless – a fabulous reputation that must be exploited. Here's a symbolic picture I don't intend to miss: Hindenburg representing the Old Germany and I the New – the old field marshall of the World War and the young corporal from the trenches pledging themselves to the swastika at the court of Frederick the Great! I'll stage such an act in Potsdam as the world has never seen! If I force a showdown now, the old idiot might resign, and I can't afford it. . . . With his prestige behind me, I can proceed step by step. I can get rid of Versailles, I can rearm, I can get allies. I don't care what they think and write about me abroad; better for them to keep underrating me until I get strong. I'll be ready to strike before they know it, the fools.

On November 9, 1923 . . . the National Socialist German Workers' Party [Nazis] was dissolved and prohibited . . . [but] today in November, 1926, it stands again free before us, stronger and inwardly firmer than ever before.

*1925*     Whoever attacks us will be stabbed from all sides. I will lead the German people in their fight for freedom, if not peacefully, then with force.

After the election of Sept. 14, 1930, in which the NSDAP won 107 seats, Hitler declared: "Do not write on your banners the word victory ... strike through the word victory and write once more in its place the word which suits us better – the word fight." -Payne

## Comments and Reaction

He was living well on borrowed money, for his only regular income consisted of small sums he received for his newspaper articles. Yet, almost immediately after leaving prison, he bought a supercharged Mercedes-Benz for 28,000 marks. -Payne

*After 1925*     The basic good of the Nazi movement remained the same: to fight "the most dreadful enemy of the German people ... Jewry and Marxism." -Bessel

Hitler's rise to power could be measured mathematically by the rising curve of unemployment. -Payne

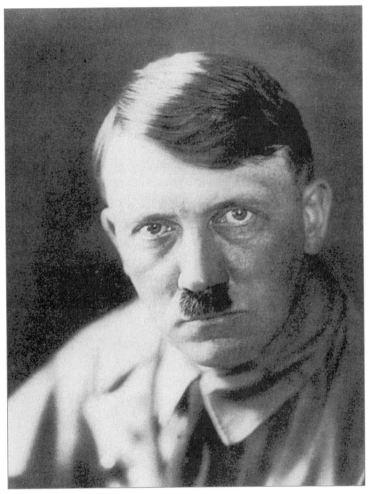

Hitler, 1930.

Before his 1925 "conversion" Joseph Goebbels said that "the insignificant bourgeois Adolf Hitler [should] be thrown out of the party."

By the time he came out of prison, Hitler had assembled the ideology of Nazism from disparate elements of anti-Semitism, pan-Germanism, eugenics and so-called racial hygiene, geopolitical expansionism, hostility to democracy, and hostility to cultural modernism. -*Evans*

"How his [Hitler's] blue eyes sparkled when his storm troopers marched past him in the light of the torches, an endless sea of flames rippling through the streets of the ancient Reich capital," noted a Hitler admirer in 1929. -*Evans*

According to Albert Speer, Hitler deliberately left his rivals to fall out among themselves while he was unavoidably detained [in jail] so that he could sweep back to take command on his own terms.

Early in their association, Goering told Hitler: I unite my faith with you and your cause. For better or for worse, I dedicate myself to you in good times and in bad, even unto death. -*Gervais*

*Birthday greetings on the leader's 37th birthday, 1926*

Dear and revered Adolf Hitler! I have learned so much from you. You have finally made me see the light. -*Goebbels*

I love you because you are both great and simple, the characteristics of genius. -Goebbels.  *Referring to Hitler in his diary*

Hitler hurled himself into the campaign . . . and between February 22 and March 12 he made nineteen speeches . . . [to] crowds ranging from 60,000 to 100,000 . . . in big cities.  *1932*

The growth of the Nazi Party coincided with the years of economic depression. -Jarman  *See Appendices B, C, & D*

Hitler is the same dear comrade. You cannot help liking him as a man . . . the born whipper-up. Together with him you can conquer the world. His most beautiful gift was the hate of our enemies whom we too hate with all our heart. -Goebbels  *1926*

He is like a child – kind, good, merciful. Like a cat – cunning, clever, agile. Like a lion – roaring and great and gigantic. A fellow – a man . . . I am his to the end . . . Germany will live. Heil Hitler. -Goebbels

No one who preaches autarchy can lead the German people to anything but ruin.
-H.V. Kaltenborn  *1932. Quoted in Payne*

"That man for Chancellor? I'll make him a postmaster and he can lick stamps with my head on them." -Paul Von Hindenberg.  *August 1932*

# Chapter 6
## Triumph: 1933 - 1936

*Dictators ride to and fro upon tigers
which they dare not dismount,
and the tigers are getting hungry.*
Winston Churchill, 1936

## Hitler Quotes

When advised that he should meet the remarkable Olympic athlete, Jesse Owens, Hitler shouted: "Do you think that I will allow myself to be photographed shaking hands with a Negro?"

I see a German Reich stretching from the North Sea to the Urals.

A retreat on our part would have spelt collapse. What saved us was my amazing aplomb. *On occupying the Rhineland, 1936*

"German people, give us four years time, then judge us." Told to Berlin crowd during Hitler's first major speech as head of state. *Feb 10, 1936*

They underestimate me because I have risen from below ... I have given them a cuff on the ear they'll long remember.

*1936*  The forty-eight hours after the march into the Rhineland were the most nerve-racking of my life. If the French had then marched into the Rhineland, we would have had to withdraw with our tails between our legs.

*Munich speech. This March 15, 1936 quote is one of his most famous.*  I go the way that Providence dictates with the assurance of a sleepwalker.

# Comments and Reaction

From March 1933 onwards, towns rushed to appoint Hitler an honorary citizen. In almost every town ... the main square was renamed Adolf Hitler Platz. -*Van Der Vat*

Hitler liked to speak about his Machergreifung meaning "seizure of power" as though he had gasped the scepter and bent Germany to his will, but in fact [used] backroom maneuvers, and gifts of millions of marks from wealthy industrialists and armament manufacturers. -*Payne*

The most fateful day of the last century [was] January 30, 1933, the day Adolf Hitler came to power. -*Black*

Ludendorf in a telegram to Hindenburg:     *1933*
"By appointing Hitler Chancellor of the Reich, you have handed over our sacred German Fatherland to one of the greatest demagogues of all time. I prophesy to you that this evil man will plunge our Reich into the abyss and will inflict immeasurable woe on our nation. Future generations will curse you in your grave for this action." -*Payne*

Hindenburg detested Hitler, but felt compelled . . . to ally himself with "that Austrian corporal." -*Collins*

The so-called "philosopher of National Socialism,"     *1933*
Martin Heidegger, told his Freiburg students that "the Führer himself and he alone is the German reality, present and future, and its law. Study to know: from now on, all things demand decision, and all action responsibility. Heil Hitler."

The Third Reich, which was spawned on January 30, 1933, was born out of the National Socialist Workers' Party (Nazis) which was the very embodiment of Adolf Hitler himself. -*Darmon*

*1933* Hitler's paper pogrom was the dull edge of the knife. The sharp edge was violence. Unrestrained acts of depraved Nazi brutality against Jews and other undesirables began at once. *-Black*

Ever since Hitler's entry into power, in 1933, the British and French Governments had conceded to this dangerous autocrat immeasurably more than they had been willing to concede to Germany's previous democratic governments. *-Liddell Hart*

Nurnburg rally, 1934.

I thank heaven for a man like Adolph Hitler, who built a front line of defence against the anti-Christ of Communism. -*Frank Buchman*

1936

By the time Hitler became Reichschancellor the SS had reached a strength of 52,000. -*Russell*

Orchestrated enthusiasm, Nurnburg 1933.

Hitler was appointed Chancellor by President Hindenburg in a strictly constitutional way and for solid democratic reasons . . . because he and his Nationalist allies could provide a majority in the Reichstag. -*Taylor*

*After 1935*    Germany had become a Führerstaat. Germany was Hitler. Hitler was Germany. And the Führer who was identical with the state could do no wrong and think no wrong. *-Remak*

Ich, Ich, Ich – The word "I" now explodes continually in his speeches. *-Payne*

After a three-day visit in June 1934 in Italy, Hitler knew he was outclassed by Mussolini, whose glittering, bemedalled uniform made Hitler's rumpled business suit look bad. Mussolini described him as a "gramophone with just seven records."

Mussolini long considered his Nazi imitator a crude, vulgar beer hall brawler with no talent for politics. Years would pass before he changed his mind. *-Gervais*

Benito Mussolini, Italian Fascist dictator, said: "I should be pleased, I suppose, that Hitler has carried out a revolution on our lines. But they are Germans. So they will end by ruining our idea."

*"I didn't like the look of him."*    On June 14, 1934 Mussolini met Hitler for the first time. The Italian dictator said: *"Non mi piace."*

Benito Mussolini, Italian dictator, once referred to Hitler as "that garrulous monk."

"The man [Hitler] is totally mad," according to Mussolini while talking with his wife, Donna Rachele. *-Gervais*

Hitler and Mussolini.

# Chapter 7
## Power & Appeasement: 1937 - 1939

*You cannot shake hands with a clenched fist.*
Mohandas Gandhi

*Every dictator is an enemy of freedom,
an opponent of law.*
Demosthenes (349-322 BC)

## Hitler Quotes

With regard to the problem of the Sudeten Germans, my patience is now at an end.

After all, who remembers today the extermination of the Armenians?

He seemed such a nice old gentleman I thought I would give him my autograph as a souvenir. *Referring to Prime Minister Chamberlain on signing the 1938 Munich Pact.*

Everlasting peace will come to the world when the last man has slain the last but one.

As the Führer and Chancellor of the German nation and the Reich, I now declare before history the incorporation of my native land into the German Reich.

We National Socialists will . . . turn our gaze to land in the East.

There can be no question of sparing Poland.

*Nov. 5, 1937 Hitler to his military commanders.*

The German army . . . and the German economy must be ready for war within four years.

Nuremburg rally

[Atrocities sink] into insignificant absurdities . . .
when measured against the mighty deeds
I perform.

[Germans must be ready] to stand firm even when
thunder rolls and lightning flashes [and] the entire
nation must stand behind the Führer as one
disciplined army.

Absolutely zero! I am telling you, absolutely zero!
-*Hitler's comment to Austrian Chancellor Schuschnigg
regarding Austria's role in history.*

I can talk peace and mean war.

I only need to give an order, and overnight all the ridiculous scarecrows on the [Austrian] frontier will vanish. *Feb. 12, 1938*

It is my unalterable decision to smash Czechoslovakia by military action in the near future. *1938*

Before us stands the last problem that must and will be solved. This is the last territorial claim I have to make in Europe, but it is a claim from which I will not recede and which, God willing, I will make good. *Referring to Sudetenland*

Post Anschluss, Vienna 1938.

Give me a kiss girls! [his secretaries] This is the greatest day of my life. I shall be known as the greatest German in history.

*March 15, 1939. Hitler speaking after his takeover of Czechoslovakia.*

The horoscope of the times does not point to peace but to war.

There's no point at all going on with negotiations. The Germans are being treated like niggers; nobody dares to treat even Turkey this way.

*Czechoslovakia, 1938*

> If Hitler had succumbed to an assassination or an accident at the end of 1938, few would hesitate to call him one of the greatest German statesmen, the consummator of Germany's history. *-Fest*

The Leader, 1939

# Comments and Reaction

Nazism was inseparable from war ... the ideology of Nazism was an ideology which regarded peace merely as preparation for war -*Bessel*

The legacy of the German past was a burdensome one in many respects. But it did not make the rise and triumph of Nazism inevitable.

From the very beginning, buildings interested Hitler mainly as statements of power. -*Evans*

If I were given a gun and told to take two shots, I would shoot Himmler, then Ribbentrop and brain Hitler with the butt of the rifle. -*Neville Henderson, British Ambassador in Berlin 1937-39.*

I am extremely anxious to see Hitler dead. -*Joseph Stalin.*

In spite of the hardness and ruthlessness I thought I saw in his face, I got the impression that here was a man who could be relied upon when he had given his word. -*Neville Chamberlain*

[Before and during the Munich appeasement] Hitler was the waiting and anxious assailant, at first inclined to robbery and later intent on murder. -Roch

There is this staggering fact that in the single year 1938 Hitler had annexed to the Reich and brought under his absolute rule 6,750,000 Austrians and 3,500,000 Sudetens, a total of over ten millions of subjects, toilers and soldiers. Indeed the balance had turned in his favour. -Churchill

> *The Moustache of Hitler*
> *Could hardly be littler*
> *Was the thought that kept recurring*
> *To Field Marshall Goering.*
>
> E.E. Bentley, "Clerihew," *Punch*, 1939

# Chapter 8
## The Man

*He was a nice man really, of course he was mad.*
Hitler's Maid servant, Gertrude

*Anyone who sees and paints a sky green and a pasture blue ought to be sterilized.*
Adolf Hitler

## Hitler Quotes

A single idea of genius is worth more than a whole lifetime of conscientious office work.

I have the gift of reducing all problems to their simplest foundations.

I might be killed by a criminal, or an idiot, at any time.

Hate is more lasting than dislike.

The only stable emotion is hate.

I am convinced that if I had been a smoker, I never would have been able to hear the cries and anxieties which have been a burden to me for so long. Perhaps the German people owe its salvation to that fact.

The new Reich will call into being an astounding blossoming of German art.

How I wish I had become an architect.

Humanitarianism is the expression of stupidity and cowardice.

It is not the neutrals or the lukewarm who make history.

*See Harclerode and Pittaway, The Lost Masters, for an excellent account of the Nazi's looting of Europe's art treasures.*

At the House of German Art in Munich, July 1937, Hitler proclaimed: "the people passing through these galleries will recognize in me its own spokesman and counselor."

Do you realize that you are in the presence of the greatest German of all time? *-Hitler speaking to Austrian Chancellor Kurt von Schuschnigg during a 1938 interview.*

Those who make history may not have a private life.

The man who is born to be dictator is not compelled. He wills it . . . there is nothing immodest about this.

But I do not need your endorsement to convince me of my historical greatness.

*Hitler speaking to Herman Rauschning*

Why do we call the whole world's attention to the fact that we have no past? -*Hitler grumbling to Himmler, whose Abnenerke - meaning something inherited from the forefathers - was a think tank whose purpose was to unearth new evidence of the accomplishments of Germany's ancestors and to convey that information to the public.*

I am one of the hardest men Germany has had for decades . . . equipped with the greatest authority of any German leader.

But if the [inner] voice speaks, I know the time has come to act.

I am the loneliest man on earth.

In perpetual peace, man's greatness must decline.

Man has become great through perpetual struggle.

*Speaking to his generals on the eve of war*

Only force rules. Force is the first law.

Close your hearts to pity! Act brutally! The stronger man is right. Be harsh and remorseless! Be steeled against all signs of compassion.

Today it seems to me providential that Fate would have chosen Braunau on the Inn for my birthplace.

*Vienna, 1938*

I believe it was God's will to send a boy from here into the Reich, to let him grow up and to raise him to be the leader of the nation so that he could lead back his homeland to the Reich.

Germany has a right to a greater living space than other peoples.

Our enemies are little worms. I saw them at Munich.

But then, that's what young men are there for [when his forces take heavy casualties].

The most sensitive part of a man is not his skin but his wallet.

Business, too, marches over corpses.
A class made up solely of intellectuals will always have a guilty conscience.

The very first essential for success is a perpetually constant and regular employment of violence.

Success is the sole earthly judge of right and wrong.

All epoch-making revolutionary events have been produced not by the written but by the spoken word.

They regard me as an uneducated barbarian. Yes, we are barbarians! We want to be barbarians! It is an honorable title.

*1933*

The intellectuals run this way and that, like hens in a poultry-yard.

Faith is harder to shake than knowledge. Love is less subject to change than respect.

True genius is always inborn and never cultivated, let alone learned ... this applies not only to the individual man but also to the race.

War is for a man what childbirth is for a woman.

Yes, I am very lonely, but children and music comfort me.

Dog lover.

I love animals, and especially dogs.

People are not to know who I am. They are not to know where I come from or about my family background.

It was with great reluctance that I had definitely to give up wearing leather shorts (lederhosen).

What is America but millionaires, beauty queens, stupid records and Hollywood.

Whenever I make a speech of great importance I am always soaking wet . . . and I have lost four or six pounds in weight.

*1933*

"Aren't you as enthralled by me as I am with you?" Hitler once asked his audience.

"It is like eating a corpse." The would-be vegetarian Hitler spoke of his loathing for meat while looking at a dish of stew.

"Look, I poach other people's countries – I don't pinch their flashlights." Hitler made this comment in jest as aides looked for a missing flashlight.

*1931*

Hitler told this joke to the Wagner Family: You all know what a volt is and an ampere, don't you? Right. But do you know what a Goebbels, a Goering are? A Goebbels is the amount of nonsense a man can speak in an hour and a Goering is the amount of metal that can be pinned on a man's breast.

*The dictator allowed no jokes about himself.*

# Comments and Reaction

The more I learn about Hitler, the harder I find it to explain. -Alan Bullock, distinguished historian.

Hitler, though technically and officially a Catholic until the day he died, was in spirit a pagan . . . It is a slander to say that the Catholic Church did not resist Hitler. -Carroll

He had the peasant's cunning, the peasant's distrust, and the peasant's strength. He was physically far more robust than he seemed to be, and he was intellectually more brilliant, and therefore more dangerous, than his enemies gave him credit for. -Payne

Hitler "lives in the midst of many men and yet he lives alone." -Michael Fry

Hitler was the product of circumstances as much as anything else. -Evans

*Reported in 1934*  If the Third Reich teaches us anything, it is that a love of great music, great art and great literature does not provide people with any kind of moral or political immunization against violence, atrocity, or subservience to dictatorship. -Evans

A young German nationalist reported that "the personality of the Leader had me totally in its spell. He who gets to know Adolf Hitler with a pure and true heart will love him with all his heart."
-Evans

It was Hitler who was celebrated above all else ... the embedding of the Hitler cult in everyday life was nowhere more obvious than in the introduction of the German greeting – Heil Hitler!

Hitler kept his personal account at the Bern branch of the Union Bank of Switzerland, and his royalties from *Mein Kampf* flowed there from 1926 to his death. *-Ziegler*

Hitler repeatedly strove to pass off his loot as legal gold. *-Ziegler*

It was they [the Swiss Bankers] who financed his (Hitler's) wars of aggression. *-Ziegler*

Hitler was one of the most evil monsters the world has ever known ... his aims were those of a maniac. *-Alexander*

Hitler's favorite movie was King Kong, and he loved Wagnerian opera, as a youth and as an adult
*-Waite*

*Ziegler strongly and eloquently demolishes the myth of Swiss neutrality. Swiss financial assistance to Hitler is fully discussed by Ziegler.*

Albert Speer, Minister of Armaments, claimed that "the dog [Blondi] remained the only living creature at headquarters who aroused any flicker of human feeling in Hitler."

He [Hitler] remains a figure that in some profound way nobody knows. -*Ron Rosenbaum.*

To most people, probably, he seems like a monstrous tyrant as one follows his bloodstained trail . . . [but] he did not seem like that to most Germans. They worshiped him and did his awful bidding. -*Shirer*

General Erwin Rommel, "the Desert Fox," privately referred to his Führer as a lunatic.

Once Hitler adopted an ideological position, even a strategic one, he adhered to it with limpet-like fixity. -*Kjelle*

The Third Reich of Adolf Hitler did not rise from some dark or evil void. The threads of its origins were woven into the very fabric of German life itself.

To his followers, Hitler had the historical personal greatness of Caesar or Napoleon.

No representation of Adolf Hitler has seemed able to present the man or satisfactorily explain him.
-*Alvin Rosenfeld, Jewish studies scholar*

He was destitute of human quality; he lacked reliability or any recognizable moral standard.
-*Darman*

Experts have determined that Hitler long suffered from the then-untreatable, progressive, post-encephalitis Parkinson's disease. -*Latimer*

As early as age forty-five, Hitler developed a tremor in his left hand. He began to hold one hand with the other or else used his left hand to grip the buckle of his Sam Browne belt when seen in public.

Hitler developed the autonomic dysfunctions characteristic of Parkinson's: abdominal distension, flatulence, heavy sweating, constipation and painful eye spasms. His rage attacks were another symptom.

Hitler would not allow doctors to examine him with his clothes off. -*Latimer*

Hitler was anxious to avoid visits to a dentist's office. His teeth deteriorated badly.

Hitler claimed that his people loved him so much that he didn't need to carry a weapon. However, many of his trousers were later found to be relined with leather pockets so he could carry a small pistol.

Hitler refused to meet the famous pilot, Charles Lindberg, because he, Hitler, couldn't match the clean-cut look of the flier.

Hitler was preoccupied with the fear of an early death. -Latimer

Hitler wanted to appear as "every man's soldier," so his uniforms avoided flash and ostentation – compared to Goering, for example.

A racing tipster who only reached Hitler's level of accuracy would not do well for his clients. -A.J.P. Taylor

Adolph Hitler is Fuehrer because he exemplifies and enshrines the will of Germany. -Winston Churchill.

His own work shows clearly enough the intellectual failings of the self and half-educated man. -Jarman

[Hitler's] face possessed an ability to express the most rapidly changing moods, at one moment smiling and charming, at another cold and imperious, cynical and sarcastic, or swollen and livid with rage. -*Bullock*

Relaxing on the Obersalzberg.

It is this mixture of calculation and fanaticism ... which is the peculiar characteristic of Hitler's personality. -Bullock

He was like a man possessed. Often moody, silent, and awkward, he would spring to life whenever the subject was mentioned [the Treaty of Versailles]. -Jarman

With Hitler, indeed, one is uncomfortably aware of never being far from the realm of the irrational. -Bullock

Hitler in a rage appeared to lose all control. His face became mottled and swollen with fury, he screamed at the top of his voice, spitting out a stream of abuse. -Bullock

Hitler cultivated [his] gift of memory assiduously. -Bullock

Hitler ... was a consummate actor, with the actor's and orator's facility for absorbing himself in a role and convincing himself of the truth of what he was saying. -Bullock

Hatred, touchiness, vanity are characteristics upon which those who spent any time in his company constantly remark. -Bullock

Hitler was as much a product of an era as he was the sum of his own inner compulsions to power, which stemmed from deeply rooted psychological problems traceable to the circumstances of his birth, childhood and upbringing. -*Gervais*

He had no feeling for literature at all, or interest in books for their own sake, but regarded them solely as a source from which he could extract material that fitted in with views he already held. -*Bullock*

Hitler always saw himself, in these day-dreams, as master of the world. -*Taylor*

The essence of the authoritarian character is the simultaneous presence of sadistic and masochistic drives. -*Fromm*

In making use of the formidable power . . . Hitler had one supreme, and fortunately rare, advantage: He had neither scruples nor inhibitions. He was a man without roots. -*Bullock*

The new ruler of Germany [Hitler] was a man of contrasts . . . he possessed great personal courage, yet he was haunted by petty fears. He was afraid of sunshine, horses, snow and water. -*Waite*

[Hitler] was one of the most effective orators in history [but] ... in private conversation he was a bore. -*Waite*

He is a genius, the natural creative instrument of fate determined by God. -*Goebbels*

Hitler, very early in his career, developed extraordinary delusions of historical grandeur by marrying his personal destiny with the course of German history. -*Overy*

He will go down in history as the most worshipped and the most despised man the world has ever known. -*Langer*

The thing he would like best is to sit in the mountains and play God, according to fellow Nazi Roehm – before he was murdered on Hitler's orders.

1934 The Führer does not change. He is the same now as he was when he was a boy. -*Goebbels*

If you try to tell him anything, he knows everything already [and] he laughs in our faces ... [and] he doesn't seem to be aware of how dishonest he is. -*Ludecke*

Hitler, from a physical point of view, is not, however, a very imposing figure — certainly not the Platonic idea of a great, fighting Leader or the Deliverer of Germany and the creator of a New Reich. In height he is a little below average. His hips are wide and his shoulders relatively narrow. His muscles are flabby; his legs short, thin, and spindly, the latter being hidden in the past by heavy boots and more recently by long trousers. He has a large torso and is hollow-chested to the point where it is said that he has his uniforms padded. From a physical point of view he could not pass the requirements of his own elite guard.

His dress, in the early days, was no more attractive. He frequently wore the Bavarian mountain costume of leather shorts with white shirt and suspenders. These were not always too clean, and with his mouth full of brown, rotten teeth and his long dirty fingernails he presented rather a grotesque picture. At that time he also had a pointed beard, and his dark brown hair was parted in the middle and pasted down flat against his head with oil. Nor was his gait that of a soldier. "It was a very lady-like walk. Dainty little steps. Every few steps he cocked his right shoulder nervously, his left leg snapping up as he did so." *-Langer*

*1938*   Writer E.A. Mowrer claimed that Hitler "seemed for all the world like a traveling salesman for a clothing firm."

*1934*   Famed wit and writer Dorothy Thompson said this about Hitler: "He is a formless, almost faceless man whose countenance is a caricature, a man whose framework seems cartilaginous, without bones. He is inconsequent and voluble, ill poised and insecure. He is the very prototype of the little man."

The world has come to know Adolf Hitler for his insatiable greed for power, his ruthlessness, his cruelty, his utter lack of feeling, his contempt for established institutions, and his lack of moral restraints. -Langer

Adolf Hitler was both brave and sincere in his promotion of his beliefs, despite the fact they were loathsome. -Roberts
How could such an unprepossessing specimen – with his absurd little moustache, rasping voice and staring eyes – have come to command such fanatical devotion? -Roberts

Hitler . . . can be accused – and indeed convicted – of being an anti-smoking, teetotal vegetarian. -Roberts

Hitler was almost entirely devoid of any but the blackest humour. -*Roberts*

Indeed, up to the age of forty, Adolf Hitler was a failure in almost every respect. -*Roberts*

Hitler radiated charisma. -*Roberts*

[Hitler] might have still been a virgin at thirty-five. -*Roberts*

Hitler [was] an excitable, garrulous creature with a vein of certifiable insanity in his composition. -*Wells*

Hitler's early opponents scorned his tactics as outright demagogy, but in everything he said or did he showed psychological insight wholly lacking in the campaigns of his [German] rivals. -*Gervais*

By virtue of his personality, his ideas, and the fact that he misled millions, Hitler poses an historical problem of the first magnitude. -*Schramm*

According to August Kubizek, boyhood friend of Hitler, Schicklegruber, Hitler's Grandmother's name, seemed to him "so uncouth, so boorish, apart from being so clumsy and impractical."

> In extremely difficult situations he has openly threatened to commit suicide. Sometimes it seems that he used this as a form of blackmail while at other times the situation seems to be more than he can bear. During the Beer Hall Putsch he said to officials he was holding as prisoners: "There are still five bullets in my pistol – four for the traitors, and one, if things go wrong, for myself." He also threatened to commit suicide before Mrs. Hansfstaengl directly after the failure of the Putsch, while he was hiding from the police in the Hanfstaengl home. Again in Landsberg he went on a hunger strike and threatened to martyr himself – in imitation of the Mayor of Cork. In 1930 he threatened to commit suicide after the strange murder of his niece, Geli . . . In 1932 he again threatened to carry out this action if Strasser split the Party. In 1933 he threatened to do so if he was not appointed Chancellor, and in 1936, he promised to do so if the occupation of the Rhineland failed. *-Langer*

According to Ernest Schenck, one of Hitler's doctors, "Hitler was psychologically dependent upon the 'idea' of drugs as magic."

A headline in a German Health Food Magazine claimed, *First Great Victory of German Vegetarians: Hitler becomes Chancellor.*

His remarkable memory, together with iron diligence and a strong power of concentration, had enabled Hitler ... to acquire knowledge of a scope and detail that again and again amazed persons ... and earned him sincere admiration. -*Schramm*

He was a strong man; and a fundamental source of his strength was hatred. Yet his hatreds did not coagulate until he was thirty years old. -*Lukacs*

*There are revisionist writers and historians. See "Admirers and Defenders, Open and Hidden" in Lukacs, The Hitler of History Ch. VIII*

Adolf Hitler was the most extraordinary figure in the history of the twentieth century ... [and] the Second World War ... was inconceivable and remains incomprehensible without him. -*Lukacs*

In fact, to a virtually unprecedented degree, he created everything out of himself and was himself everything at once: his own teacher, organizer of a party and author of its ideology, tactician and demagogic savior, leader, statesman, and for a decade the "axis" of the world. -*Fest*

He stands like a statue, grown beyond the measure of earthly man. -*Newspaper description of Hitler*

*Nov. 9, 1935*

105

[Hitler's] lifelong mania for record size, speed, and numbers was characteristic of a man who had never managed to overcome his youth with its dreams, injuries, and resentments. -*Fest*

# Chapter 9
## Racism

*Blood, sin and desecration of the race are
the original sin in this world and the end
of a humanity which surrenders*
Adolf Hitler

## Hitler Quotes

The mulatto children came about through rape or the white mother was a whore. In both cases, there is not the slightest moral duty regarding these offspring of a foreign race.

The Americans ought to be ashamed of themselves for letting their medals be won by Negroes.

The contamination by Negro blood on the Rhine in the heart of Europe [will] . . . deprive the white race . . . through infection with lower humanity.

All those who are not racially pure are mere chaff.

*When Jesse Owens, a black American track star won three Olympic medals in Berlin, 1936, Hitler refused to be present when the medals were awarded.*

The Nordic race has a right to rule the world.

A stronger race will drive out the weaker ones ... to give their place to the strong.

The race question is the key not only to world history but to human culture itself.

What we must fight for is to safeguard the survival and growth of our race and nation; is to feed its children and to maintain the purity of the blood.

To disregard the laws of our blood is to deny God's order in this world and to violate his command.

The fight against Jewish world Bolshevization requires a clear attitude toward Soviet Russia. You cannot drive out the Devil with Beelzebub.

*He later called Churchill "a hopeless square-snout."* Adolf Hitler often used such expressions as "filthy trash from the East," "the swinish pack of parsons," "the crippled dung art," and referred to Jews as "this vilest sow's brood that ought to be beaten to a pulp."

It is no accident that the first cultures arose in places where the Aryan, in his encounters with lower people, subjugated them and bent them to his will.

*Vienna*

I was repelled by the conglomeration of races which the capital showed me, repelled by this whole mixture of Czechs, Poles, Hungarians, Ruthenians, Serbs, and Croats, and everywhere, the eternal parasitic fungi of humanity – Jews and more Jews. To me the giant city seemed the embodiment of racial desecration.

Our nation's only true possession is its good blood.

All the great cultures of the past perished only because the originally creative race died out from blood poisoning.

All eugenic progress can begin only by eliminating the inferior and by insisting on proven blood.

Germanic Laws on marriage and eugenics can be understood only if they are seen for what they are: Eugenic laws.

If we were to divide mankind into three species; the culture-creators, the culture-bearers, and the culture-destroyers, only the Aryan would be likely to fit into the first definition.

# Comments and Reaction

Hitler's all-encompassing ideology of race was a vulgarized version . . . of Social Darwinism. -*Carroll*

For the nightmare of Hitler's ideas and racism "to become a lived reality," tens of thousands of Germans had to perform criminal deeds willingly, sometimes even quite eagerly. -*Crew*

According to Hitler's conviction, a people had the right to exist only if it were racially valuable. If it were, then it also had the right to expand at the expense of weaker peoples. That this amounted to "subjugation" did not even occur to Hitler; in his view "subjugation" did not exist in the realm of nature. -*Schramm*

# Chapter 10
## Anti-Semitism

*Anti-Semitism ... is the swollen envy of
Pygmy minds – meanness, injustice.*
Mark Twain

*Anti-Semitism is a useful revolutionary expedient.
My Jews are a valuable hostage given
to me by democracy.*
Adolf Hitler

## Hitler Quotes

Wherever I went I began to see Jews, and the more I saw, the more sharply they became distinguished in my eyes from the rest of humanity. I began to hate them. I became an anti-Semite. *Vienna*

The German republic is "a corrupt racket run by the Jews at the expense of the national interests." *1923*

|||
|---|---|
| Vienna | When thus for the first time I recognized the Jew as the cold-hearted, shameless, and calculating director of this revolting vice traffic in the scum of the big city, a cold shudder ran down my back. |
| | I didn't know what to be more amazed at: the agility of their tongues or their virtuosity at lying. Gradually I began to hate them. |
| | I had at last come to the conclusion that the Jew was no German. |
| | Not until my fourteenth or fifteenth year did I begin to come across the word "Jew" with any frequency. |
| | [The Jew] always talks about the equality of all men ... those who are dumb begin to believe that. |
| | The New Testament is a Jewish swindle on the part of four Evangelists. |
| 1921 | The solution of the Jewish question could only be solved by brute force. |
| 1923 | We know that if they [Jews] come to power, our heads will roll in the sand. |

Russia has been a plague-centre for mankind...
for if the state tolerates a Jewish family among it,
this would provide the core bacillus for a new
decomposition.

Conscience is a Jewish invention. It is a blemish,
like circumcision.

In the year 1916-17 nearly the whole production
was under the control of Jewish finance.

The Jews have no organizational ability, but are
a forment of decomposition.

For us there are only two possibilities: either we
remain German or we come under the thumb of
the Jews. This latter must not occur; even if we are
small, we are a force. A well organized group can
conquer a strong enemy. If you stick close together
and keep bringing in new people, we will be
victorious over the Jews.

The Jew has not grown poorer: he gradually gets
bloated, and, if you don't believe me, I would ask
you to go to one of our health resorts; there you
will find two sorts of visitors: the German who goes
there, perhaps for the first time for a long while, to
breathe a little fresh air and to recover his health,
and the Jew who goes there to lose his fat.

*Speech,*    And the right has further completely forgotten
*Apr. 12, 1922*    that democracy is fundamentally not German: It is Jewish. It has completely forgotten that this Jewish democracy with its majority decisions has always been without exception only a means towards the destruction of any existing Aryan leadership.

*Speech,*    Internationalization today means only Judaization.
*Sep. 18, 1922*    We in Germany have come to this: that sixty-million people sees its destiny to lie at the will of a few dozen Jewish bankers.

*Speech,*    No salvation is possible until the bearer of
*Sep. 18, 1922*    disunion, the Jew, has been rendered powerless to harm.

*Speech,*    We demand immediate expulsion of all Jews who
*Apr. 13, 1923,*    have entered Germany since 1914, and of all those,
*Munich*    too, who through trickery on the Stock Exchange or through other shady transactions have gained their wealth.

*Speech,*    Why have the Jews been against Germany? That is
*Sep. 18, 1922,*    made quite clear today – proved by countless facts.
*Munich*    They used the age-old tactics of the hyena – when fighters are tired out, then go for them!

As early as 1923 Hitler claimed that escalating inflation was part of a Jewish plot. He added: "According to the Protocols of Zion, the people are to be reduced by submission by hunger."

The Jew has never founded any civilization, though he has destroyed hundreds ... Everything he has is stolen ... [and] he seeks to disintegrate the national spirit of the Germans and pollute their blood.

The most powerful antipode to the Aryan is the Jew ... [who] is and remains the typical parasite, a sponger who, like a malign bacillus, spreads more and more as long as he will find some favorable feeding ground.

The Jewish people are bound together in a conspiracy to rule the world.

Only a knowledge of the Jews provides the key with which to comprehend the inner, and consequently real, aims of Social Democracy.

Later I often grew sick to my stomach from the smell, of these caftan-wearers. Added to this was their unclean dress and their generally unheroic appearance.

*The infamous Protocols of the Elders of Zion, first published in Moscow in 1903, was the work of Sergei Nilus, an unscrupulous Russian Monk. He was commissioned by Czar Nicholas II to forge a collection of documents to 'prove' that a mysterious Jewish group called "the Wise Men of Zion" planned to conquer the world. Hitler believed the false account to be true.*

Was there any form of filth or profligacy . . . without at least one Jew involved in it?

If you cut even cautiously into such an abscess, you found, like a maggot on a rotting body, often dazzled by the sudden light – a kike!

The fact that nine tenths of all literary filth, artistic trash, and theatrical idiocy can be set to the account of [the Jewish] people, constituting hardly one hundredth of all the country's inhabitants . . . was the plain truth.

*Nazi sign, 1934*    "Whoever buys from a Jew is a Traitor".

A thirty-centimeter shell has always hissed more loudly than a thousand Jewish newspaper vipers - so let them hiss.

This Jewification of our spiritual life and mammonization of our mating instinct will sooner or later destroy our entire offspring . . .

The mightiest counterpart to the Aryan is represented by the Jew.

In the Jewish people the will to self-sacrifice does not go beyond the individual's naked instinct of self-preservation.

If the Jews were alone in this world, they would stifle in filth and offal.

The Jew possesses no culture-creating force of any sort...

[The Jew was always] a parasite in the body of other peoples.

The Jew has always been a people with definite racial characteristics and never a religion.

How far the inner Judaization of our people has progressed can be seen from the small respect, if not contempt, that is accorded to manual labor.

With Satanic joy in his face, the black-haired Jewish youth lurks in wait for the unsuspecting girl which he defiles with his blood, thus stealing her from her people.

The Jew is the great master in lying, and lies and deception are his weapons in struggle.

Only the Jew can praise an institution which is as dirty and false as he himself. *e.g. parliament*

Jewish finance ... desires not only the complete economic annihilation of Germany, but also her complete political enslavement.

The Jew today is the great agitator for the complete destruction of Germany.

[Listen] to the hissing of the Jewish world hydra. With astute shrewdness they knead public opinion and make it into an instrument for their own future.

Today it is not princes and princes' mistresses who haggle and bargain over state borders; it is the inexorable Jew who struggles for his domination over the nations.

In Russian Bolshevism we must see the attempt undertaken by the Jews ... to achieve world domination.

[The Jews] activities produce a racial tuberculosis among nations.

In the year 1918, there was no such thing as organized Anti-Semitism ... [and] our first efforts at revealing the true enemy to the people appeared to be almost hopeless at the time ...

*Nazi doctors played a leading part in the scientific justification of Hitler's racist views.*

Now the Jews know only too well that in his thousand years of adaptation he may have been able to undermine European people and train them to be raceless bastards.

Once I am really in power, my first and foremost task will be the annihilation of the Jews.

*Hitler told a journalist this in 1922.*

# Comments and Reaction

Anti-Semitism was a consistently exploited organizing principle, a pillar of Protestant and Catholic identity. -Carroll

The genocide of Jews as the work of [Hitler's] Nazism, not Christianity ... [and] the Final Solution was a contradiction of everything Christianity stands for. -Carroll

Hitler read the phony Protocols of the Wise Men of Zion and was fascinated by its discussion of the political intrigue, deception, lies, subversion and conspiracy supposedly planned by Jews in their search for world power.

*James Carroll claims that the Holocaust "throws many things into relief – the human capacity for depravity, the cost of ethnic absolutism, the final inadequacy of religious language and of silence."*

*The Protocols are still being reprinted by the tens of thousands.*

In response to the Protocols, Hitler claimed they were instructive, because he and his followers could copy those methods – their way, of course. He added: "We must beat the Jew with his own weapon."

When reading of the conspiracy of the Jews set forth in the Protocols, one can easily believe he/she is reading Hitler's own political ideas.

When Hitler was decorated with the Iron Cross, First Class on August 14, 1918, the man who pinned it on his uniform was First Lieutenant Hugo Gutman, a Jew.

[For Hitler] the Jew became the inevitable ... scapegoat for the Great War and everything else that was wrong with Germany. -*Darmon*

The killing of the Jews was not the result of the bureaucratic processes of a dictatorship going berserk ... but an official crime deliberately staged by Hitler. -*Kjella*

Hitler wanted to "unify a chosen people who had never been politically one. He would purify their race. He would make them strong. He would make them lords of the earth."-*Shirer*

Hitler was obsessed with Jewry since his impoverished youth in Linz and Vienna.
-*Van Der Vat*

Hitler refers to Jews as maggots, a pestilence, parasites, a vampire and the personification of the devil as the symbol of all evil. *-Roeloff*

# Chapter 11
## Education, Propaganda, & Symbolism

*The foundation of every state is the
education of its youth.*
Diogenes

*The first task of propaganda is to win people
for subsequent organization; the first task
of organization is to win men for the
continuation of propaganda.*
Adolf Hitler

## Hitler Quotes - Education

A class made up of solely intellectuals will always have a guilty conscience. What luck for the rulers that men do not think.

Universal education is the most corroding and disintegrating prison that liberalism has ever invented for its own destruction.

A violently active, dominating, intrepid, brutal youth – that is what I am after . . . I want to see in its eyes the gleam of pride and independence, of prey. I will have no intellectual training. Knowledge is ruin to my young men.

I begin with the young. We older ones are used up . . . but my magnificent youngsters! Look at these men and boys! What material! With them I can create a new world.

Compulsory military style labor for males 18 years old, 1934.

It is important to bring every member of the new generation under the spell of National Socialism in order that they may never be spiritually seduced by any of the old generation.

My pedagogy is hard. The weak must be chiseled away... I want a violent, arrogant, unafraid, cruel youth who must be able to suffer pain. I want my young people strong and beautiful and... athletic.

*An official journal of education in Hitler's Germany claimed that Mein Kampf, the immortal work of the Leader, is our infallible pedagogical guiding star.*

German girls keeping fit.

*Speaking to the Hitler Youth*

We have to learn our lesson: one will must dominate us, we must form a single unity; one discipline must weld us together; one obedience, one subordination must fill us all, for above us stands the nation.

*Sep. 1928*

Our people must be delivered from the hopeless confusion of international convictions and be educated consciously and systematically to fanatical nationalism.

We must educate the people to fight against the delirium of democracy and bring it again to recognition of the necessity for authority and leadership.

We must deliver the people from the atmosphere of pitiable belief in reconciliation, understanding, world peace, the League of Nations and international solidarity.

*Hitler was known to be prejudiced against professors.*

If the German professor were to be put in charge of the world for a few centuries, there would be nothing but cretins running around after a million years — gigantic heads with hardly any bodies at all.

# Comments and Reaction

German children were taught in school to report any conversation by their parents that was against Hitler's regime.

*The young pianist Karl Kreiten was beheaded for treason because he said that "Hitler is losing the war." A family friend repeated his comment.*

Enthusiastic Hitler Youth.

*From the Hitler Youth Anthem written by Baldur von Schirach.*

We march for Hitler through the night and suffering ... our flag means more to us than death.

Hitler claimed that the child belonged to the state, and the sole object of education is to train tools for the state.

The Nazis viewed education as just another form of political propaganda. -Halleck

*Oath spoken by the new members of Jungvolk or Hitler Youth, every April 20: Hitler's Birthday.*

I promise
In the Hitler Youth
to do my duty
at all times
In love and faithfulness
to the Führer
So help me God.

*"Chant" uttered by members of Hitler Youth.*

Now we will fight against Hell itself for our Leader. Heil Hitler! Sieg Heil.

# Hitler Quotes - Propaganda & Symbolism

The broad mass of a nation ... will more easily fall victim to a big lie than to a small one. Propaganda does not have to state the truth objectively ... but must serve its own interests uninterruptedly.

Only constant repetition will finally succeed in imprinting an idea on the memory of a crowd.

I have never delivered a firebrand speech.

All epoch-making revolutionary events have been produced not by the written but by the spoken word.

If you wish the sympathy of broad masses, then you must tell them the crudest and most stupid things.

[Propaganda] should never admit a glimmer of doubt in its own claims, or concede the tiniest element of right in the claims of the other side.

Let us pledge ourselves at every hour, on every day, only to think of Germany, of Volk and Reich, of our great nation. Our German Volk, Sieg Heil!

It is possible by means of shrewd and unremitting propaganda, to make people believe that heaven is hell – and hell, heaven.

The Volkswagon . . . is the car of the future.

1914-1918  Propaganda in the War was a means to an end . . . the existence of the German people.

The receptivity of the great masses is extremely limited, their intelligence is small, their forgetfulness enormous.

[Propaganda] must be addressed always and exclusively to the masses.

The function of propaganda does not lie in the scientific training of the individual, but in calling the masses' attention to certain facts.

All propaganda must be popular, and its intellectual level must be adjusted to the most limited intelligence among those it is addressed to.

The art of propaganda lies in understanding the emotional ideas of the great masses and finding . . . the way to the attention . . . [and] heart of the broad masses.

All effective propaganda must be limited to a very few points and must harp on these slogans until . . . the public understands what you want.

[Propaganda's] task is to serve our own right, always and unflinchingly.

The masses are then in no position to distinguish where foreign injustice ends and our own begins.

The people in their overwhelming majority are so feminine by nature and attitude.

[Propaganda] must confine itself to a few points and repeat them over and over.

In the field of propaganda we must never let ourselves be led by aesthetes or people who have grown blasé.

The purpose of propaganda is not to provide interesting distraction for blasé young gentlemen [but] . . . to convince the masses.

The masses are slow moving . . . and only after the simplest ideas are repeated thousands of times will the masses finally remember them.

A slogan must be presented from different angles, but the end of all remarks must always and immutably be the slogan itself.

Propaganda must be adjusted to the broad masses in content and in form, and its soundness is to be measured exclusively by its effective result.

An agitator who demonstrates the ability to transmit an idea to the broad masses must always be a psychologist, even if he were only a demagogue.

The supporter is made amenable to the movement by propaganda.

Propaganda does not, therefore, need to rack its brains with regard to the importance of every individual instructed by it.

Propaganda tries to force a doctrine on the whole people.

Propaganda works on the general public from the standpoint of an idea and makes them ripe for the victory of this idea.

If propaganda has imbued a whole people with an idea, the organization can draw the consequences with a handful of men.

In every really great world-shaking movement, propaganda will first have to spread the idea of this movement.

Propaganda had the effect that after a short while hundreds of thousands not only believed us to be right but desired our victory, even if personally they were too cowardly ... to fight it.

As director of the party's propaganda I took much pains ... to prepare the soil for the future greatness of the movement.

The psyche of the broad masses is accessible only to what is strong and uncompromising ... the masses prefer a ruler to a suppliant.

I shall give a propagandist cause for starting the war: never mind if it be plausible or not, the victor shall not be asked afterwards whether he told the truth or not. Words build bridges into unexplored regions.

Propaganda has "no more to do with scientific accuracy than a poster has to do with art. The greater the mass of men to be reached, the lower its intellectual level must be."

# Comments and Reaction

Hitler's genius lay in his unequaled grasp of what could be done by propaganda, and his flair for seeing how to do it. -Bullock

His employment of verbal violence, the repetition of such words as smash, force, ruthless, hatred, was deliberate. -Bullock

Hitler was at the center of Nazi visual propaganda. Pictures of Hitler appeared on stamps, postcards, and in booklets. Hitler was on billboards. Hitler was in newsreels. Framed photos of Hitler were given as Christmas gifts. This visual assault was part of . . . the Hitler myth. -Crew

Hitler had a natural genius for mob oratory and had realized that the way to get results was to pitch the message on an emotional rather than an intellectual level, and gear it to the most stupid elements of the audience. -Collins

His tongue was like a lash that whipped up the emotions of his audience. -Langer

Any definition of this [Nazi] movement, this ideology, this phenomenon, which did not contain the name Hitler would miss the point. -Kjelle

Nazi Propaganda Poster

1923   Hitler has the advantages of a man who knows theatre only from the gallery. *-Bertolt Brecht*

By what can only be termed an evil stroke of genius, he gave the Nazi movement a flag, a symbol, in the form of the ancient swastika cross ... [which] took on a strange fascination for numbers of Germans, who flocked under its banner. *-Shirer*

Aesthetic politics symbolism and choreography, Munich 1935.

Hitler's swastika became "a twentieth-century shorthand for evil." -*Crew*

Hitler chose the female form of the ancient swastika emblem as his symbol, and planned the design of the Nazi flag, which he described as "something akin to a blazing torch," -*Darman*

Hitler had grasped as no one before him what could be done with a combination of propaganda and terrorism. -*Bullock*

To attain the objectives set by his soaring ambition, Hitler proposed to use three methods: propaganda, diplomacy, and force. -*Gervais*

Clearly, Hitler understood oratory as melodramatic theatre . . . [and] his shouting could rattle windows in their frames. -*Fuchs*

*Virginia Cowles, American journalist, attended a Hitler rally where 200 000 people heard Adolf Hitler speak:*

As the time for the Führer's arrival drew near, the crowd grew restless. The minutes passed and the wait seemed interminable. Suddenly the beat of the drums increased and three motorcycles with yellow standards fluttering from their windshields raced through the gates. A few minutes later a fleet of black cars rolled swiftly into the arena: in one of them, standing in the front seat, his hand outstretched in the Nazi salute, was Hitler.

Then Hitler began to speak. The crowd hushed into silence, but the drums continued their steady beat. Hitler's voice rasped into the night and every now and then the multitude broke into a roar of cheers. Some of the audience began swaying back and forth, chanting 'Sieg Heil' over and over again in a frenzy of delirium. I looked at the faces around me and saw tears streaming down people's cheeks.

*-Overy*

# Chapter 12
## Hitler & Women

*Verily the best of women are those
who are content with little.*
Mohammed (570-632)

*Women should remain at home, keep house,
and bear and bring up children.*
Martin Luther (1483-1546)

## Hitler Quotes

I can never marry because my life is dedicated to my country.      *1924*

Hitler stated: "The masses are my bride."

Hitler said "how very much I too would like to have a family, children, children! . . . but I have to deny myself this happiness, I have another bride – Germany.

*1929* I love Geli and could marry her. But you know my views. I am determined to remain a bachelor.

Geli Raubel

The world of the woman is the man. Only now and then does she think of anything else.

A man has to be able to stamp his imprint on any woman. As a matter of fact, a wife does not want anything else.

Adoring women after Rhineland success, 1936.

## Comments and Reaction

Hitler's "love," Geli Raubal, his half-niece, apparently took her own life. Hitler was devastated and spent an evening weeping at her grave.

*Sep. 19, 1931*

Hitler soon became a familiar figure among the more well-to-do of Munich, especially among the women of advanced age who seemed positively enchanted by him. Usually he'd give the hostess a big bouquet of roses and, as he kissed her hand, he'd bow in the exaggerated Viennese style. When he talked to women, he'd even change his voice. While often harsh and guttural, his voice became smooth and he affected a Viennese accent. During conversation, he gave each woman the impression that he was completely captivated by her and her alone. Though most women expected some kind of ruffian, they were swept away when they suddenly discovered themselves alone with a charmer.
"I simply melted away in his presence," said Mrs Bruckman. -*Schwarzwaller*

Four women attempted suicide over the dictator. Three succeeded.

The appeal [in post WWI War Germany] of right-wing extremism to women proved no less potent than it was to men. -*Evans*

The National Socialists praised the heroic racially pure unmarried mother's loyalty to the Führer. -*Koonz*

A pretty girl maneuvered Hitler under the mistletoe and kissed him. Heinrich Hoffman wrote: "I shall never forget the look of astonishment and horror on Hitler's face. Hitler stood there biting his lip in an effort to master his anger." -Toland

*New Year's Eve, 1925*

> Although some persons close to Adolf Hitler believed that he died a virgin, West German historian and biographer Werner Maser claimed Adolf Hitler had an 18-month love affair with a French peasant girl while he was stationed as a German army corporal in the village of Wavrin, France during WWI. In 1918, while in a military hospital, Hitler learned that Charlotte had given birth to his son, whom she named Jean Marie. When the Germans occupied France in 1940, Hitler had the Gestapo locate Jean Marie Loret and give him a high-ranking position in the French police administration. Presently, Hitler's son is an unemployed railway worker living in St. Quentin, France.
>
> -Irving Wallace et al, The Book of Lists #2.

"From the first moment when I heard of Adolf Hitler, he gave me a new faith, he brought me strength and power and love. He is my idol, and I will devote my life to him," said a woman whose marriage failed because of her commitment to Hitler.

1935 Women faint, when, with face purpled and contorted with effort, he blows forth his magic oratory. -Newsweek

As far as the German people know he has no sex life [which is seen] as a great virtue. -Langer

1933 He will never marry a woman since Germany is his only bride. -Ernst Franz Hanfstaengl

An American psychoanalyst concluded that Hitler achieved sexual satisfaction by having women defecate and urinate on him.

In 1926 when he was 37 years old he became infatuated with a 16 year old girl named Mary Reiter who declined his request for a kiss. -Fuchs

It is claimed that Hitler, at age of sixteen, fell in love with a girl named Stefanie. However, he didn't have the nerve to approach her.

August Kubizek claimed that young Hitler wrote "innumerable love poems" to Stefanie. In one, she appeared "as a damsel of high degree, dressed in a dark-blue, flowing velvet robe and riding upon a white palfrey over flower-strewn meadows, her loose tresses falling over her shoulders like a golden flood. A bright spring sky overhung the scene. All a pure radiant happiness."

Hitler courted Henny Hoffman, the teenage daughter of Heinrich Hoffman, the photographer who took the famous 1914 crowd picture. The girl gratified Hitler's "masochistic perversion" and told her father about it. The father was given the exclusive right to take and license photos of Hitler. It made the father a fortune. *-Fuchs*

It is claimed that Hitler had a relationship with Jenny Haug, a sister of one of his chauffeurs.

It is also claimed that one Renate Mueller found herself naked in a bedroom with a naked Hitler. The story continues: She was asked to give Hitler "punishment" which greatly excited him. Renate repeatedly kicked the German leader, and used a leather whip on him. *-Fuchs*

*Unity's sister Diana was married to the British fascist leader, Oswald Mosley.*

In 1935, Hitler met Unity Valkyrie Mitford, who had come from England to Munich to study language. The dictator kissed her hand and asked about her studies. Her reply: "Mr. Hitler, I am not only a university student but also an English fascist." The day Germany and England went to war, Unity fired a bullet into her head. With Hitler's help, she recovered, and he transported her to England via neutral Switzerland.

Eva Braun, jealous of Unity, took thirty-four powerful sleeping pills. The would-be suicide failed because the Jewish physician Dr. Marx saved her life with gastric washing.

*1936* Hitler supplied a house for Eva Braun and her sister, Gretl. He supplied a bodyguard and gave Eva a Mercedes with a full time driver.

Some observers claim that Eva Braun looked very much like Hitler's mother.

Lack of female company [in prison] had never bothered Hitler . . . and at the age of thirty-five, he may well have been a virgin. -*Stone*

Many women, including the most devoted "horizon tales" in Prussia, attempted Hitler's virtue. -*Stone*

In Vienna young Hitler talked for hours on end about the dark and perverted aspects of sex. -*Schwarzwaller*

In November 1922, Hitler became acquainted with Ernst "Putzi" (Cutie) Hanfstaengl who had just returned to Germany from USA. Putzi was a kind of unpaid press secretary for Hitler, who dated Putzi's sister, Erna. Hitler and Erna were frequently seen together in fine restaurants.

*Hitler adored Putzi's wife, Helen.*

Hitler's associates also knew how strongly he reacted to beautiful and cultivated women. -*Schramm*

Hitler was always unfailingly gracious and correct with women. -*Schramm*

Hitler felt that premarital intercourse was not objectionable, but rather it assured that a man and his "maiden" really belonged together. -*Schramm*

Dr. Otto Strasser cared for Angelika (nicknamed Geli) the daughter of Hitler's half-sister, Angela Raubal. Strasser did not approve of the Adolf-Geli romance because Hitler was nineteen years older than the girl and that "he was a sadist and a masochist, both in one person". -*Schwarzwaller*

> At first, Hitler put his niece up in the Klein Boarding House at English Garden where Rudolf Hess had also been living after the war. Then he got her a room at 43 Thiersch Street, in the house next to his own apartment. Hitler was with Geli every day. One could see them in the Hick Cafe, in the Stephanie Cafe, in the Carlton Tea Room, in the Osteria or in the Prinzregenten Cafe, near the Brown House where Hitler was supervising the remodeling job.
>
> Everybody knew that the relations between the uncle and niece went beyond mere kinship. There were even whispers that Hitler intended to marry Geli. A marriage of this sort would not have been unusual for the family - Hitler's father had also married his niece.
>
> Hitler showered the girl with presents. He bought her furs and jewels and tried to anticipate her every wish. *-Schwarzwaller*

Winifred Wagner rejected Hitler's marriage proposals in the early 1930's because she was repulsed by his unorthodox sexual demands.

Joseph and and Magda Goebbels tried discreetly to find attractive women for Hitler. Among them was Gretl Slezak, the 30 year old daughter of opera singer Leo Slezak. She was the bosomy type of woman Hitler preferred. *Schwarzwaller*

"Renate Mueller at that time was one of Hitler's favorites. She certainly would not have been disinclined to enter into a sexual relationship with the Führer . . . she had gladly accepted his invitation to come to his private apartment in the Reich Chancellery, expecting an evening of love-making. When she got there, they both undressed. But instead of jumping into bed with Renate Mueller, Hitler threw himself on the floor before the actress and begged her to beat him and stomp on him. Horrified, she refused. He continued to insist, imploring her to do him this favor. She said that he then humiliated himself before her with the worst self-accusations and groaned that he was her slave and was unworthy of being in the same room with her. In the process, he became very excited. She finally gave in, stepping on him, beating him with his riding crop and, upon his request, heaping obscene insults on him. Hitler, she reported, became increasingly excited and finally started to masturbate. -*Schwarzwaller*

Leni Riefenstahl (1902-2003), often loathed for her links with Adolf Hitler, made *The Triumph of the Will* one of the most powerful films in the history of the cinema. Her documentary film of the 1933 Nazi party made her reputation. During most of her long life the actress, director, and dancer remained fascinated by the personality of the dictator – even long after his death. As an elderly woman she said that being "sorry is not enough [and] there is no word for what I feel" about her connection to Hitler. Riefenstahl also made a remarkable film about the 1936 Berlin Olympics. She knew how to capture the pageantry so much a part of the Nazi rallies.

*Hitler chose the film's title.* Leni Riefenstahl's film *The Triumph of the Will* was a popular and accepted expression of Nazi ideology.

Leni Riefenstahl.

# Chapter 13
## Leadership & the Big Lies

*The shepherd always tries to persuade the sheep that their interests and his own are the same.*
Stendhal (1783-1843)

*The art of leadership ... consists in consolidating the attention of the people against a single adversary and taking care that nothing will split up that attention.*
Adolf Hitler, 1925

## Hitler Quotes - Leadership

Above all, a man who feels it is his duty ... to assume the leadership of his people is not responsible to the laws of parliamentary usage.

German compatriots, my German workers, if today I am speaking to you and to millions of other German workers, I have a greater right to be doing this than anybody else.

*Berlin, Nov. 10, 1933*

The victor will not be asked afterwards whether he told the truth or not. When starting and waging war it is not right that matters, but victory.

Confusion, indecision, fear: these are my weapons. The one means that wins the easiest victory over reason: terror and force.

The majority can never take the place of the man.

1934 [We want] to create a state to which every German can cling in love ... to find laws which are commensurate with the morality of our people [and] to install an authority to which each and every man submits to joyful obedience.

1934 Our leadership ... lives in the people, feels with the people, and fights for the sake of the people.

No power on earth can shake the German Reich now. Divine Providence has willed it that I carry through the fulfillment of the Germanic task.

A clever conqueror will impose his demands on the conquered in installments.

Who is not with me will be crushed.

Essentially all depends on me ... because of my political talents.

*Hitler on the eve of going to war.*

The state must have the personality principle anchored in its organization.

The doom of a nation can be averted only by a storm of glowing passion, but only those who are passionate themselves can arouse passion in others.

The conviction of the justification of using even the most brutal weapons is always dependent on ... a fanatical belief in the necessity of the victory.

I have an old principle only to say what must be said to him who must know it, and only when he must know it.

The whole work of Nature is a mighty struggle between strength and weakness – an eternal victory of the strong over the weak ... [and] through all the centuries force and power are the determining factors.

*The statement is one example of Hitler's crude Darwinism.*

We want to make a selection from the new dominating case [which] has the right to dominate others because it represents a better race.

*1930*

*1923* It is not an economic question which now faces the German people, it is a political question – how shall the nation's determination be recovered?

*After the reoccupation of the Rhineland* My pride is that I know no statesman in the world who with greater right than I can say that he is the representative of his people.

[The individual] must realize that the freedom of the mind and will of a nation are to be valued more highly than the individual's freedom of mind and will.

*1937* The main plank in the National Socialist programme is to abolish the liberalistic concept of the individual and the Marxist concept of humanity and to substitute for them the Volk community, rooted in the soul and bound together by the bond of its common blood.

We have to put a stop to the idea that it is a part of everybody's civil rights to say whatever he pleases.

When I first came to power in 1933, years of the most difficult struggle lay behind me . . . I had to reorganize everything, from the people itself to the armed forces.

German boy, do not forget you are a German, and little girl, remember that you are to become a German mother.

Public relations at work.

Terrorism is an effective tool. I shall not deprive myself of it merely because these simple-minded bourgeois "softies" take offense... People will think twice before opposing us, if they know what awaits them in the camps.

The churches may take command of the German in the hereafter. The German nation, through its Fuehrer, takes command of the German in this world.

1934 In this hour I was responsible for the fate of the German people, and thereby I became the supreme Justiciar.

He who would live, let him fight, and he who would not fight in this world of struggle is not deserving of life.

I see struggle as the fate of all living creatures. No one can escape it, unless he wishes to be defeated.

The humbler the people are, the greater the craving to identify themselves with a cause bigger than themselves.

1925 Whoever attacks us will be stabbed from all sides. I will lead the German people in their fight for freedom, if not peacefully, then with force.

Confident leader on parade.

It must be quite unique in history for someone like me to have got so far.   *1939*

I owe it to that period of life that I grew hard and am still capable of being hard.   *In Vienna*

Woe to the weak!

Without the army we [Nazis] would all not be here; all of us once came out of that school.

In daily life the so-called genius requires a special cause, indeed, often a positive impetus to make him shine!

The hammer-stroke of Fate which throws one man to the ground suddenly strikes [places] steel in another.

The great leader girding for war, will concentrate on a single image of the enemy, however many enemies there are.

*Speech, Apr. 13, 1923, Munich* — Always before God and the world the stronger has the right to carry through what he wills.

*Speech, Apr. 24, 1923, Munich* — Where then can any strength still be found within the German people? It is to be found, as always, in the great masses: There energy is slumbering and it only awaits the man who will summon it from its present slumber and will hurl it into the great battle or the destiny of the German race.

*Speech, Nov. 23, 1926, Essen* — World history, like all events of historical significance, is the result of the activity of individuals – it is not the fruit of majority decisions.

We want to be the supporters of the dictatorship of national reason, of national energy, of national brutality and resolution. Germany can be saved only through action, when through our talking here the bandage has been torn from the eyes of the last of the befooled ... then we shall see which is the stronger; the spirit of international Jewry or the will of Germany.

*Speech, Aug. 1, 1923, Munich*

The orator.

*Speech, Sep. 14, 1936, Nurnburg* — I have won my successes simply because in the first place I endeavoured to see things as they are and not as one would like them to be; secondly, when once I had formed my opinion I never allowed weaklings to talk me out of it or to cause me to abandon it; and thirdly, because I was always determined in all circumstances to yield to a necessity when once it had been recognized.

*Speech, Oct. 5, 1938, Berlin* — What I have achieved in these six years was possible only because I had standing behind me the whole German people.

Mustn't our principle of parliamentary majorities lead to the demolition of any idea of leadership?

There is no principle which, objectively considered, is as false as that of parliamentarianism.

In world history the man who really rises above the norm of the broad average usually announces himself personally.

[In parliament] why are five hundred chosen when only a few possess the necessary wisdom to take a position in the most important matters, and this is the worm in the apple.

Such an institution can only please the biggest liars and sneaks.

*Parliament*

The world is not for cowardly peoples.

The progress and culture of humanity are not a product of the majority, but rest exclusively on the genius and energy of the personality.

The prerequisite for the creation of an organizational form is and remains the man necessary for its leadership.

Leadership itself requires not only will but also ability . . . and most valuable of all is a combination of ability, determination, and perseverance.

The great mass of the people cannot see the whole road ahead of them without growing weary and despairing of the task.

But it would be absolutely mistaken to regard a wealth of theoretical knowledge as characteristic proof for the qualities and abilities of a leader.

For leading means being able to move masses.

The combination of theoretician, organizer, and leader in one person is the rarest thing . . . [and] this combination makes the great man.

Diplomacy must see to it that a people does not heroically perish, but is practically preserved.

The psyche of the great masses is not receptive to any half measure or to weakness.

Chapter heading in *Mein Kampf* – "The strong man is mightiest alone. One should never forget that nothing truly great in this world has been won by coalitions. Success is only achieved by the individual conqueror."

I am the drummer of the German people. I beat out the march for which their feet are waiting. [Hitler, referring to the April 20, 1920 moment when "his" movement changed its name to National Socialist German Workers' Party: NSDAP.]

He who would be a leader shall have the highest, unlimited authority; he also shall bear the final and heaviest responsibility.

The enormous difference between the tasks of the theoretician and the politician is also the reason why a union of both in one person is almost never found.

Oppressed territories are led back to the bosom of a common Reich, not by flaming protests, but by a mighty sword.

*i.e. "formerly German" territories*

The man who is born to be a dictator is not compelled. He wills it. He is not driven forward, but drives himself. — The man who feels called upon to govern a people has no right to say "If you summon me, I will co-operate. No! It is his duty to step forward."

*Hitler speaking at his 1924 trial.*

# Hitler Quotes - The Big Lies

The size of the lie is a definite factor in causing it to be believed, for the vast masses of a nation are in the depths of their hearts more easily deceived than they are consciously and intentionally bad. The greater the lie, the greater the chance it will be believed.

National Socialism does not harbor the slightest aggressive intent towards any European nation.

*1935*

Something therefore always remains and sticks from the most impudent lies.

The victor will never be asked if he told the truth.

When you lie, tell big lies ... in the big lie there is always a certain force of credibility because the broad masses of a nation are always more easily corrupted.

The broad mass of a nation ... will more easily fall victim to a big lie than a smaller one.

## Comments and Reactions

What Germany was lacking [before his leadership] was a close cooperation of brutal power and ingenious political intention.

The Third Reich was not a static or monolithic dictatorship; it was dynamic and fast-moving, consumed from the outset by visceral hatred and ambitions. Dominating everything was the drive to war. *-Evans*

In time, Hitler began to believe that he was divinely chosen to save Germany from Jews and Marxists and preserve it for Aryan magnificence. -Kjelle

For most of the Henchmen, in one way or another, Hitler filled their need for a "savior," a God-like human they could personally worship and publicly obey. -Kjelle

Adolf Hitler never doubted that the world could be seen in only one way – his way. -Kjelle

[Hitler's] stamina was derived from his monstrous egotism, the blind self-confidence that made him believe himself a man of destiny, chosen by an act of providence to lead the Nordic world. -Darman

The major question . . . is not what personality traits allowed an "unknown corporal" of the Great War to become the all-powerful leader Adolf Hitler, but rather why tens of millions of Germany's blindly followed him to the end. -Friedlander

Without Hitler's uncanny ability to grasp and magnify the basic urges of such a mass craving for order, authority, greatness, and salvation, the techniques of propaganda alone would not have sufficed. -Friedlander

In Hitler's parlance "to render harmless" meant killing. -Friedlander

1919    As in a dream everything suddenly became clear [to Hitler]. Germany had been stabbed in the back and clawed down by the Jews, by the profiteers and intriguers behind the front, by the accused Bolsheviks . . . shining before him he saw his duty, to save Germany from these plagues . . . and lead the master race to its long-decreed destiny. -Churchill

*Oath of allegiance to Hitler taken by his military officers*    I swear by God this holy oath that I will give unlimited obedience for the Führer of the German Reich, Adolf Hitler.

Hitler was used to dealing with mediocrities. -Payne

Hitler held his Henchmen in a firm grip. They carried out what he decided. -Kjelle

After their first meeting, Goebbels wrote to Hitler: "Like a rising star you have appeared before our wondering eyes. You perform miracles to clear our eyes." -Kjelle

The hallmark of Adolf Hitler's power was destruction. -Kershaw

Hitler's secret political police, could never have done its bloody work without the help of literally tens of thousands of ordinary Germans. -*Crew*

Hitler was an egocentric psychopath who had the German people in his complete control. -*Latimer*

Blind trust – that was the characteristic which Hitler chiefly valued in his followers. -*Jarman*

Surprise was a favorite gambit of Hitler's, in politics, diplomacy and war. -*Bullock*

[Schacht claimed that] Hitler often did find astonishingly simple solutions for problems ... his solutions were often brutal, but almost always effective. -*Bullock*

Hitler believed vehemence, fanaticism and passion were "the great magnetic forces which alone attract the masses." -*Gervais*

Absolute power corrupted him, as it does all who hold it. -*Shirer*

Hitler did not know any foreign countries at first hand. He rarely listened to his foreign minister ... [and] he judged foreign states – men by intuition. -*Taylor*

Hitler was by temperament a revolutionary who had no intention of restoring the traditional stiff, class-conscious, backward-looking hierarchical society to which many German nationalists looked back with regret. -Bullock

*Up to 600 000 such patients were put to death by the Nazis*

In a note to a Nazi doctor Hitler wrote: [You] are authorized to extend the responsibilities of physicians still to be named in such a manner that patients whose [mental] illness ... is incurable, can be granted release by euthanasia.

One of Hitler's most bitter critics wrote; "I have been asked many times what is the secret of Hitler's extraordinary power as a speaker. I can only attribute it to his uncanny intuition ... He enters a hall. He sniffs the air ... his words go like an arrow to their target." -Bullock

When he was confirmed by the party as Führer, he presented himself as living proof that personality, not aptitude, wealth or title, was the key to supreme political leadership. -Overy

Hitler harnessed two of the most powerful, if vicious, of human emotions – envy and resentment – to his chariot wheels, and they took him an astoundingly long way. -Roberts

Next comes Hitler himself: Hitler is a man without compromise. Above all he knows no compromise with himself. He has one single thought that guides him: to resurrect Germany. This idea suppresses everything else. He knows no private life. He knows family life no more than he knows vice. He is the embodiment of the National will.

It would be an oversimplification to characterize Hitler as a Hyper-Machiavellian no longer inhibited by law. His concept of legality came from what he saw as "the eternal laws of natural events." He recognized codified laws only to the extent that they agreed with these "eternal" laws – he felt entirely justified in overthrowing or violating the law when it did not yet correspond to the "eternal" law. *-Schramm*

The knighthood of a holy goal which can be climaxed by no man: Germany! ... Hitler ... surprises [with] his geniality. The tranquility and strength radiate, almost physically, from this man. In his presence others grow. How he reacts to everything ... His features harden and the words drop as stones ... The classical solemnity with which Hitler and his surrounding group of co-workers consider their mission has very few parallels in world history. *-Langer*

[Hitler] belongs in the company of Genghis Khan, Tamerlane, Stalin and Mao Tse-tung, inhuman megalomaniacs all. -*Roberts*

Hitler neither understood nor was he interested in economics. But he was neither ignorant nor disinterested in the social and political consequences of the world depression. -*Gervais*

[The "Night of the Long Knives"] . . . showed that the new Master of Germany would stop at nothing. -*Churchill*

*He later did.* I owe all I am to Hitler. How can I betray him? -*Heinrich Himmler*

We are all creatures of the Fuehrer. His faith makes us the most powerful of men. -*Hermann Goering*

Adolf Hitler, I love you because you are both great and simple. These are the characteristics of the genius. -*Joseph Goebbels (diary)*

Hitler wanted to be seen as impulsive, emotional, inspired. In fact, he was a cool manipulator who carefully planned for maximum effect. -*Fuchs*

History records no phenomenon like him. -*Fest*

Hitler was the consummate dissembler, capable of many poses, but all observers agree that to see him unleashing his hatred for Jews, to see him barking his threats, this was to see truly into the spitting cauldron of his soul. -*Fuchs*

Adolf Hitler was a figure of either heroic creativity or satanic destructiveness. But to people who saw him close-to, he was prosaic. -*Stone*

He lived for power. -*Stone*

His subordinates, while sometimes energetic enough, were chosen for their obedience, not their intelligence. -*Stone*

No one else produced, in a solitary course lasting only a few years, such incredible areolation in the pace of history. No one else so changed the state of the world and left behind such a wake of ruins as he did. -*Fest*

We know that he was an extraordinary demagogue able to play on the sensitivities of the masses with breathtaking virtuosity, mesmerizing listeners with his infectious conviction that he could not fail ... we know of his elementary instinct for power and his utter ruthlessness in exercising it. -*Schramm*

At the age of forty, Hitler had come to terms with life. He was a very lonely man, but he was prepared to settle for a long romance with power. -*Stone*

# Chapter 14
## The Politician

*Tyranny is a habit, it has capacity for development, it develops finally into a disease.*
Fedor Dostoevsky (1921-81)

*Dictators always look good until the last minute.*
Thomas G. Masaryk (1850-1937),
Czechoslovakia's first President

## Hitler Quotes

The state is a means to an end. Its end lies in the preservation . . . of a community of physically and psychologically homogeneous creatures.

The essential thing is the formation of the political will of the nation: that is the starting point for political action.

The very first essential for success is a perpetually constant and regular employment of violence.

We do not intend to abolish the inequality of all men ... [but rather] create insurmountable barriers which would turn it into law.

Pacifism is simply undisguised cowardice.

*The Treaty of Versailles, 1919*

Not only have I united the German people politically but I have also rearmed them. I have endeavoured to destroy, sheet by sheet, that treaty which in its 448 articles contain the last vilest oppression which peoples and human beings have ever been expected to endure.

Any alliance whose purpose is not the intention to wage war is senseless and useless.

The acquisition of land for colonization ... could be achieved only with bloodshed, but the goal must be worth the bloodshed.

Concentrate upon one adversary, and focus the people's hatred upon this enemy.

*4 months before Hitler became chancellor.*

Possible foreign complications give me headaches.

Germany is the bulwark of the West against Bolshevism

The steady labor of the German plow . . . merely needs to be given land by the sword.

The sole political party existing in Germany is the National Socialist German Workers' Party (Nazis).

*Article I Law Against the New Formation of Parties of July 14, 1933, signed by Chancellor Adolf Hitler, among others.*

Declarations of neutrality can be ignored.

Peace treaties whose demands are a scourge to nations [often] strike the first roll of drums for uprising to come.

I became the supreme justice of the German people. Everyone must know for all future time that if he raises his hand to strike at the state, then certain death is his lot.

Mutinies are repressed in accordance with laws of iron, which are essentially the same.

Dictatorship is justified if the people declare their confidence in one man and ask him to lead.

For every problem, that causes unrest today goes back to the defects of the [Versailles] Peace Treaty.

Only an adequately large space on this earth assures a nation of freedom of existence.

Every healthy, unspoiled nation therefore sees the acquisition of new territory not as something useful but as something natural.

What is basic ... is that Germany truly sees the destruction of France as a means to an end, which is to enable our nation subsequently to expand elsewhere at long last.

The foreign policy of the national Socialist (Nazi) movement ... will always be a policy of space.

Politics is a woman. Love her unhappily and she will bite off your head.

A new age of magic interpretation of the world is coming.

In his own way he [Stalin] is a hell of a fellow.

1924  Instead of working to take power by force, we must hold our noses and enter the Reichstag.

Generally speaking, a man should not take part in politics before he has reached the age of thirty.

Vehemence, passion, fanaticism, these are "the great magnetic forces which alone attract the great masses."

The people in their overwhelming majority are so feminine in their nature that sober reasoning motivates their thoughts and behavior far less than feeling and emotion.

And thus the left is forced more and more to turn to Bolshevism. In Bolshevism they see today the sole, the last possibility of preserving the present sate of affairs. They realize quite accurately that the people are beaten so long as Brain and Hand can be kept apart.

*Speech, Apr. 12, 1922*

Certainly a government needs power, it needs strength. It must, I almost say, with brutal ruthlessness press through the ideas which it has recognized to be right, trusting to the actual authority of its strength in the state.

*April 12, 1922*

If a people is to become free it needs pride and will power, defiance, hate, hate, and once again hate.

*Speech, April 10, 1923*

Even today we are the least loved people on earth. A world of foes is ranged against us and the German must still today make up his mind whether he intends to be a free soldier or a white slave.

*Speech, April 10, 1923*

The only possible conditions under which a German state can develop at all must therefore be: the unification of all Germans in Europe.

| | |
|---|---|
| *Speech,*<br>*Apr. 24, 1923* | Communists on principle reject the discipline imposed by the state; in its stead they preach party discipline: they reject the administration bureaucracy of their own movement. |
| *Speech,*<br>*Aug. 1, 1923* | Our movement was not formed with any election in view, but in order to spring to the rescue of this people as its last help in the hour of greatest need, at the moment when in fear and despair it sees the approach of the Red Monster. |
| *Speech,*<br>*Sep. 14, 1936,*<br>*Nurnburg* | I can come to terms with a Weltanschhauung [bolshevism] which everywhere as its first act after gaining power is not the liberation of the working people, but the liberation of the scum of humanity, the asocial creatures concentrated in the prisons. |
| *Sep 14, 1936* | Communism Bolshevism turns countrysides into sinister wastes of ruins; National Socialism transforms a Reich of destruction and misery into a healthy State and a flourishing economic life. We can pass by the lying Marxist shouts in silence [because] to them lying is just as vitally necessary as catching mice for a cat; their function [controlled] by its masters, the Jews. |

# Comments and Reaction

Hitler, as an early politician, "showed a marked preference for the spoken over the written word." -*Bullock*

In the early days of Nazism, Hitler showed a political genius. -*Roper*

In replacing class with race, and the dictatorship of the proletariat with the dictatorship of the leader, [Hitler's] Nazism reversed the usual terms of socialist ideology. -*Evans*

The vast expansion visualized by Hitler in *Mein Kampf* would take place principally at the expense of Russia.-*Gervais*

Throughout his dark career, Adolf Hitler displayed a remarkable ability to survive political defeat and reemerge, his power intact and even enhanced. *Darmon*

For all his elected successes, there had never been any doubt that Hitler came into office as the result of a backstage political intrigue. The Germans did not elect Hitler Reich Chancellor, Nor did they give their . . . approval to his creation of a one-party state. -*Evans*

Anticommunism had always been fundamental to Hitler's ideology and to his rise to power. -Payne

Hitler apparently believed that "Italians had a subordinate place in Nazi racial hierarchy." -Payne

In principle and doctrine, Hitler was no more wicked and unscrupulous than many other contemporary statesmen. In wicked acts he outdid them all. -Taylor

"Better Hitler than Communism" was the phrase which opened the way for Hitler first within Germany, and then on a wider scale in Europe. -Taylor

Hitler enjoyed meeting foreign statesmen face to face for it gave him the opportunity to discern their weaknesses. -Payne

What ultimately made Hitler a formidable political threat, however, was his ability to mask brutal fanaticism behind a facade of conventionality whenever that served his purposes. -Turner

# Chapter 15
## Religion

*There can be no surer sign of decay in a country than to see the rites of religion held in contempt.*
Niccolo Machiavelli (1469-1527)

*To all things clergic, I am allergic.*
Alexander Woolcott (Attributed)

## Hitler Quotes

[Protestants] are insignificant little people, submissive as dogs, and they sweat with embarrassment when you talk to them.

We shall have no other God but Germany.

National Socialism is a form of conversion ... once we hold power, Christianity will be overcome ... and a new Germany without the Pope and the Bible will be established.

Christianity is a religion for slaves and fools ...
I am a liberating man from the degrading chimera known as conscience.

Hitler and religious leaders.

> The religions are all alike ... that will not stop me from tearing up Christianity root and branch and annihilating it in Germany.

*Hitler speaking on July 20, 1933 about the Concordat with the Vatican.*

> I shall certainly not make martyrs of them ... I shall tear the mask of honesty from their faces [and] ... make them [Catholic priests who oppose him] appear ridiculous and contemptible.

*Speech, Apr. 12, 1922*

> I say: my feeling as a Christian points me to my Lord and Saviour as a fighter. It points me to the man who once in loneliness, surrounded only by a few followers, recognized these Jews for what they were and summoned men to fight against them and who, God's truth, was greatest not as a sufferer but as a fighter.

# Comments and Reactions

The Catholic Church is faulted for its silence in the face of the Final Solution, even for its tacit sponsorship of the virulent anti-semitism that drove the machinery of genocide. -Carroll

*The author of these words is an ex-priest, novelist, and historian who calls himself an "amateur Catholic"*

The peculiar evil of Adolf Hitler was not predictable, nor was Christianity his only antecedent. He was as much a creature of the [earlier] racist, secular, colonizing empire builders ... as he was of the religion into which he was born, and which he parodied. -Carroll

Hitler considered Islam, with its simple theology and ethos of holy war, the best of the major religions. -Payne

Bishop Berning claimed that "the German bishops have long ago said Yes to the new [Nazi] state, and have not only promised to recognize its authority ... but are serving the state with burning love and all our strength."

*Sep. 21, 1933*

Saar party leader Alois Spaniel described Hitler as "a new, greater and more powerful Jesus Christ." Church leader Hans Kerrl described Hitler as the "real Holy Ghost."

               Hitler has very little admiration for Christ, the Crucified. -*Langer*

1937      Hamburg's Mayor claimed: "We need no priests or parsons. We communicate direct with God through Adolf Hitler. He has many Christ-like qualities."

*April 1937*    A Rhenish group of so-called Christians claimed: "Hitler's work is God's law, and the decrees and laws which represent it possess divine authority." -*Langer*

               The first commandment of Hitlerian morality was therefore the preservation of the collective vital force of the German people; and misgivings of an older culture were simply brushed aside. -*Schramm*

# Chapter 16
## North American Responses

*The ultimate failures of dictatorship
cost humanity far more than any
temporary failures of democracy.*
Franklin D. Roosevelt, 1937

*Do you think Der Führer could
keep on being Der Führer,
If he saw what every body else sees
every time he looks in the mührer?*
Ogden Nash

## Hitler Quotes

The German Reich is bound together by chains, but the British Empire is held together only be moonbeams.

I wish that I could send some of my shock troops to Chicago and other big American cities to help in the elections. We look to Heinrich Ford as the leader of the growing Fascist movement in America.

*It is claimed that Hitler put Henry Ford's picture on his desk.*

Everything about the behavior of American society reveals that it is half judaized, and the other half negrified. How can one expect a state like that to hold together?

1933 Hitler said: "we shall soon have an S.A. [Storm Trooper] in America." He claimed that U.S.A. could become an ally once the Nazis undertook overseas expansion.

Later, Hitler changed his mind about the U.S.A. The reason was that the country was rotten and weak, and had too many "inferior races": Jews and Blacks.

Hitler talked about building huge bombers which would cross the Atlantic Ocean and "blitz" New York. Nothing came of that idea.

## Comments and Reactions

1937 Canadian Prime Minister William L. McKenzie King wrote in his diary that Hitler was "a calm, passive man, deeply and thoughtfully in earnest." King said: "I will stake my belief in Hitler's word that the people themselves do not want war, and that he, himself, has primarily the interests of the people at heart."

King wrote in his diary about Hitler: "He impressed me as a man of deep sincerity and a genuine patriot."

*Mar. 27, 1938*

King wrote to Adolf Hitler: "You, I believe, can do more than any man living today to help your own and other countries along the path to peace and progress."

*Jun. 30, 1937*

King claimed: "I looked him right in the eye when I told him, 'If you don't watch out, you'll have Canada against you in the event there is a war.'"

The Second World War descended upon Canada when depression was still the chief public topic. -A.R.M. Lower

The Nazis . . . took the whole thing and turned it into a Jew, and started slaughtering them. *-James Reaney*

*Regarding the "scapegoat" idea*

Hitler promised his followers the sky and the stars . . . when people are depressed and hungry, such promises bring hope and are not questioned. He also restored Germany's national pride. The defeated people were now told that they were supermen, destined to rule the world. *-Donald C. Willows & Stewart Richmond*

By 1935 Hitler "der Führer," had a grip on the German nation matched by no other leader in German history . . . [and] soon had the nation on the march. -*Willows & Richmond*

Capt. Truman Smith – "A marvelous Demagogue!" -*Payne*

Adrien Arcand, Canadian Nazi leader, 1930's.

King predicted that he [Hitler] would not risk a large war. -*Hutchinson*

Canadian Prime Minister McKenzie King had been the appeaser of the appeasers ... and had judged Hitler ... as a simple peasant who wanted nothing outside Germany [but] began to see the part he must play. -*Hutchinson*

[King had an] amazing miscalculation of Hitler, whom he met and described as a harmless and rather stupid peasant. -*Hutchinson*

The impression which King formed of the Fuehrer was one not only absurd but calamitous. -*Hutchinson*

On the eve of Munich, King had not quite lost faith in his original diagnosis of the diseased mind [Hitler's] now engulfing Europe in its fantasies. -*Hutchinson*

In a telegram to British Prime Minister Chamberlain after Munich, King stated, "the heart of Canada is rejoicing tonight at the success which has crowned your unremitting efforts for peace [with Hitler]." -*Ramsay Cook*

After Munich, John Wesley Dafoe, Canadian journalist giant asked: "What's the cheering for?"

Major Scott giving Nazi salute.

How many divisions has McKenzie King? Not Adolf Hitler's words but perhaps his thoughts, opined by C.P. Stacey

Shortly after the Munich conference, Herbert Hoover, ex-President of USA, said that "there is more realistic hope of military peace for the next few years than there has been for some time."

One cannot help feeling that the whole European panorama is fundamentally blacker than at any time in your lifetime or mine.
-President F.D. Roosevelt .

*Letter to the U.S. Ambassador to France, 1936*

We cannot build walls around us and hide our heads in the sand. -F.D. Roosevelt

*1935*

When Hitler forced Americans to take anti-Semitism seriously, it was apparently felt that the most eloquent reply that could be made was a dead silence. -Henry Popkin

This translation is so expurgated as to give a wholly false view of what Hitler is and says.
-F.D. Roosevelt

*On an abridged edition of* Mein Kampf, *1933*

In 1937, Hitler created a new medal, the Cross of the German Eagle Order. The first American recipient was the automobile maker Henry Ford. The American disavowed his earlier anti-Semitism. Flyer Charles Lindberg also received the medal.

Joseph P. Kennedy, U.S. Ambassador to the Court of St. James, and father of the Kennedy "clan," told Hollywood's fifty leading motion picture men that their "products" should not refer to the troubles suffered by Jews in Germany. The reason: Any war that could begin would be seen by Americans as "A Jewish War."

# Chapter 17
## After Words

Young Hitler loved to play cowboys and Indians. He enjoyed "wild west" stories.

When a child, Hitler was subject to violent temper tantrums; as a dictator he was famous for them.

By the time Hitler first reached Vienna, he was a German nationalist.

Hitler's adolescence produced political prejudices that lasted to the end of his life.

At the outbreak of war, Hitler was an unathletic, haggard, sickly young man of twenty-five. The social loner, however, blossomed in the beer halls and common rooms. *1914*

The twenty-one-year-old Adolf Hitler saw a movie in Vienna called "The Tunnel," about a labour revolt at a construction project. The revolt's leader was an inspiring orator. Hitler was impressed with the power of his words. *1910*

To Hitler, the outbreak of war in 1914 was a liberation from the monotony and aimlessness of his life.

Hitler was a brave soldier, but his fellow soldiers considered him odd and a loner. On August 14, 1918, he was awarded the Iron Cross, First Class "for personal bravery and general merit."

*See Appendix E* Two million of the thirteen million of Germany's armed forces were killed between 1914 and 1918 – one death for every thirty-five citizens of Germany. Left were more than 500 000 widows, and one million children without fathers.

During WWI, Corporal Hitler was very subservient to his officers. Later, while meeting with royalty, aristocrats, and wealthy industrialists, he was also subservient.

Hitler hated the Weimar Republic because he considered it weak. He admired the military and industrial leaders because they represented power.

*See Appendix A* The 1920 program of the NSDAP, written by Hitler and two colleagues, was a masterpiece of demagogy whose main points became the unalterable planks of the Nazis' platform.

Hitler was somewhat intrigued by the Ku Klux Klan, so he sent Kurt Ludecke to the USA to investigate the possible usefulness of the movement. Hitler learned that the Klan was not sufficiently well organized or ruthless enough to be a Nazi "partner."

*1924*

Hitler's Nazism institutionalized terror.

Nearly a dozen attempts were made on Hitler's life between 1933 and 1939. Those attempts failed without so much as a shot being fired. At least six of the would-be assassins were beheaded.

As he planned, Hitler took office legally, and not by revolution.

Some experts argue that if Germany had a long and strong democratic tradition, Hitler would not have come to power.

Marinus van der Lubbe, a young Dutch Communist, "helped" Hitler's cause: the demented man supposedly set fire to the Reichstag on February 27, 1933, thus providing Hitler with a reason to suspend key civil liberties in Germany. The fire was possibly started by the Nazis themselves.

*The Reichstag Fire Decree*

*The first Reich, or Holy Roman Empire, spanned 962 - 1806, & the second Reich from 1871 - 1919.*

Hitler prophesied his Third Reich would last one thousand years.

Rearmament for Germany was Hitler's first overt breach of the Treaty of Versailles.

In 1932 Hitler denounced the coming 1936 Berlin Olympics as "an invention of Jews and Freemasons." Later he welcomed the games by saying "if Germany is to stand host to the entire world her preparations must be complete and magnificent." Hitler, who attended the games wearing a military style Nazi Party uniform, had himself named "patron and protector" of the games.

*Cf. Hitler Youth; the Duped Generation, H.W. Koch*

Adolf Hitler's first European conquests were bloodless. Diplomacy, not the sword, was his tool.

Other than Hitler, who else in history grasped the power that emerged when terrorism and propaganda merged?

It would be wrong to suggest that if Hitler "had stopped" after what he had achieved by 1938, he would have to be considered one of the greatest German leaders. Such a view ignores Hitler's program, methods, character, and personality.

A question demanding a complex answer:
How and why did the world's statesmen ignore the warnings that Hitler included in his *Mein Kampf* for over a decade?

Hitler's "infallible intuition" made him "the greatest military commander of all time" – according to him.

Hitler shrewdly guessed that the Allies would not stop his illegal rearming or his successful attempts to gain territories populated by Germans, e.g. Austria and Sudetenland (Czechoslovakia).

Hitler once planned to change the name of Berlin to Germania.

Hitler had great capacity for self-delusion.

Until the very end of his life, Hitler retained the gift of magnetism which defies description and analysis.

Seldom, if ever, did Hitler let his guard down. He was secretive, wary, and had great distrust for others.

Hitler loved fast, powerful automobiles, flowers in his room, dogs, certain sweets, and pretty but unclever women.

*Norman Cousins wrote that the book was "one of the most extraordinary historical documents of all time."*

Hitler, a vegetarian, did not smoke, and seldom drank.

Hitler wore spectacles in his office but never in public.

Hitler did not like to be photographed wearing glasses.

Hitler lied when he claimed he read 7000 military books.

Hitler liked to be photographed with animals and children – never quite kissing the youngsters.

There was one art that Hitler regarded as predominately his own: the art of the Law Giver.

Hitler was embarrassed to undress before a doctor. He swore that he'd never be photographed while wearing bathing trunks. He feared that a forger would "set" his head on another body wearing bathing trunks. He refused to have a masseur.

Hitler believed tobacco represented the wrath of North American Indians who wanted revenge for having been given hard liquor.

Hitler took malicious pleasure in other people's mistakes and misfortunes.

Early in his life, Hitler was alienated from other people, and could easily dispense with their company. Their happiness, sorrows and ambitions meant little if anything to him.

Hitler, a vegetarian, was plagued by a paranoiac fear of cancer and by a real heart condition.

Hitler had a photographic memory; he had a remarkable memory for figures, numbers, maps, military details, and events.

Adolf Hitler could barely drive an automobile, could play the piano a bit, and used an elastic exerciser to keep in shape.

Many of Hitler's contemporaries thought that away from the microphone and the stage, he was rather an unimpressive individual.

Hitler had trouble sleeping, so on many evenings he gathered followers, secretaries, and toadies who received his talk about everything under the sun, a virtual monologue. He slept late, but the others could not.

Hitler worried about dying early, before he could complete his work.

Clausterphobic Hitler had the elevator leading to his Austrian mountain nest mirrored so that it would appear larger and more open.

Many experts claim that Hitler did not have the capacity to love anyone deeply.

Hitler often referred to the masses as "an empty-headed herd of sheep."

One man's personality, that of Adolf Hitler, dominated a modern society as never before. The Bohemian corporal's demonic, bizarre personality and political genius were unique in modern times.

Hitler's rudeness, arrogance, and boorishness highlighted his personality.

Adolf Hitler was an astute, cynical politician whose charisma added to his style of leadership. He was also a consummate actor and a compulsive fanatic.

Hitler's daily routines were followed to the extreme. He was careful about his clothing. He brushed his teeth and washed his hands frequently. He was very clean, bathed often, hated smoking and drinking, and lived as a vegetarian.

Hitler, who took himself seriously, was extremely sensitive to ridicule. He was a great mimic.

Hitler liked to present himself as a great authority and lover of "good music."

It is likely that the heavyset, tall Hindenburg, moustache and all, reminded Hitler of his father – the parent who was "so cruel" to him. Hitler had little respect for Hindenburg, his senior.

*The poison that Goebbels, his wife, and their six children used to commit suicide was first tested on Blondi.*

Hitler, the prolific murderer, loved dogs. There is a famous 1935 photograph of Hitler and his Alsatian named Muck. Another Alsatian bitch, Blondi, was later given to Hitler by Martin Borman.

Hitler was a habitual liar, and it is entirely possible he invented stories about close calls [as a soldier].

Hitler's collar and shoulders were often flecked with dandruff.

When meeting someone for the first time Hitler stared with what he believed was a penetrating gaze.

There is a common myth that Hitler was short. In fact, he was nearly five feet, ten inches tall. Other sources claim he was much shorter.

Many people consider Hitler's personality to be the basis of his appeal.

The dictator would not completely disrobe while being "checked over" by a doctor. Hitler inclined to hypochondria.

Hitler usually showed contempt for those who served him.

Hitler often claimed that his first name was a contraction of two old German words: *Altha* and *Wolfa*, which mean Noble Wolf. (Later, his field headquarters were named by him, e.g. Wolf's Lair, Wolf's Glen, and Werewolf.)

Hitler's interest in cars was one of the few things which could distract him from his politics. For the sake of streamlining, Hitler told the Porsche car company that the peoples' car "should look like a beetle."

Initially, Hitler wanted the car to be *Kd7-Wagen*, which was a contraction of words meaning "Strength Through Joy." Germans scornfully used *Kd7-Kotz durchs Fenster* which means "Vomit Through the Window." The Volkswagon cars eventually emerged in 1938, but they were not available to the public.

The rumour was spread that Hitler was a *"teppich fresser"* which means carpet chewer. The false rumour had Hitler throwing himself to the floor in a violent rage – and then chewing on the carpet. Hitler chewed his fingernails and often sucked his fingers.

Hitler worried about his weight and once said "imagine me going around with a pot belly."

The dictator entertained some visitors with vocal impressions of cars and other machinery. He could accurately mimic the sound of machine gunfire, a howitzer, and artillery fire.

He ate a lot of pastry and candy. Chocolates were his favorite treat. A friend claimed that "teetoller" Hitler sometimes put sugar in a glass of wine. The friend claimed that Hitler usually put seven teaspoons of sugar in his tea.

Hitler had a great fear of being poisoned.

Smoking was forbidden in Hitler's presence.

Hugo Blaschke, Hitler's American-trained dentist, said that because the German leader consumed so much sugar, his teeth were rotten and yellow. Many of his teeth were replaced with porcelain or gold.

Some of Hitler's contemporaries claimed that he wore an "armored hat" lined with three-and-a-half pounds of steel. It is also claimed that Hitler's upper body seemed bulky because he often wore a bullet proof vest.

Hitler was a consistent movie fan. On some nights he watched two or three movies.

Hitler refused to dance, but on occasion he picked out tunes on the piano. He also played the flute and a harmonica.

Hitler's greatest musical capability was as a whistler. He could "reproduce" long passages from Wagner and other composers.

Hitler received generous payment for the frequent articles he wrote, and required the Party's newspapers to publish them. He was also paid for having his picture on postage stamps.

In the basement of his Chancellery, Hitler had a powerful toy cannon used to knock down wooden soldiers painted with the uniforms of Russia, England, Poland, and France. When visiting there, Mussolini also enjoyed playing with Hitler's toy.

In Hitler's Germany, Blacks and homosexuals were to be eliminated. In the new order, there was no place for Gypsies (Romani) and most Slavs.

The first Nazi proposal to rid Germany of the "Gypsy Menace" was presented in 1933. Twenty thousand Romani were to be sent out to sea, and the ships sunk. The plan was abandoned.

Many Romani were sterilized because they were wrongly accused of being mentally defective.

Other Romani men who earlier served in the German armed forces were removed from their units only to be gassed in Auschwitz.

At least half a million Romani were murdered by the Nazis. Up to 15 000 homosexuals perished in the camps.

Hitler hated many lawyers and professors.

Hitler was very aware of his pictorial image.

*Other Native Americans were not mentioned.*

The word "Aryan" as used by Hitler finally lost all rational meaning. The Japanese had to be declared Aryan when they became allies. A Nazi journalist was found to have a North American Sioux Indian grandmother. After 1938, deliberations the Nazi Chamber of the Press ruled that the Sioux Indians were officially Aryan.

Hitler's obsession with race was tied to his confusion between race and nationality.

There is no doubt that Hitler believed what he said about Jews. Anti-Semitism was a major theme of his career.

During the 1936 Olympics in Berlin, Adolf Hitler ordered that barracks living quarters have signs mounted over toilets reading "Dogs and Jews are not allowed."

*The signs were removed after pressure from Olympic officials.*

*Kristallnacht* featured Nazi anti-Jewish demonstrations, which destroyed twenty-nine warehouses, and eight-hundred-fifteen shops. Fires were set to one hundred ninety-one synagogues and one hundred seventy-one dwellings, with seventy-six other buildings completely destroyed by fire.

*Nov. 9-10, 1938*

Though less than 1% of Germans were Jews, Hitler held the Jews accountable for most of the troubles suffered by Germans.

Adolf Hitler never hid his attitude towards the Jews or his intention to exterminate them.

The Nazis knew what appealed to kids – sharp uniforms, bright flags, marching music, weapons, and tales about heroes.

The Hitler Youth organization did not tolerate individuality or originality; of all the characteristics required by Hitler's henchmen, ruthlessness was the most important.

Hitler Youth and the cult of personality.

The 1936 anthem for German Olympic youth had its purpose: "the Fatherland's chief gain / the Fatherland's highest demand / in necessity: Sacrificial death."

Hitler's SS wore hats bearing a silver death's head, a touch which symbolized "duty until death."

The myth created around his image was one of the most formidable propaganda instruments of the third Reich.

Hitler imposed his will on Europe's best educated people, the Germans.

Despite an unpleasant and strident voice, Hitler was a persuasive, powerful orator aided by an effective, efficient propaganda apparatus.

Radio was the Nazi Party's most effective means of mass communication.

For the flag, he chose red, the revolutionary color, to provoke the left; in the center he placed a white circle; and inside it he put the swastika, in black.

Schools were fundamental for setting up the Nazis' propaganda and cultural machinery.

Hitler at a Girls' School.

Hitler and his personal photographer worked together to present the right image. The dictator preferred to be photographed in modest military-like uniforms.

Some Nazi leaders made direct comparisons between Jesus Christ and Hitler, drawing intense criticism from church leaders.

By the early 1930s there seemed to be a need to soften Hitler's image, so pictures were taken of children and Hitler together.

The Nazi "propaganda machine" was headed by the Minister of Propaganda, Goebbels, who ran an efficient group of some 300 civil servants and 500 other employees.

In the swastika, chosen by Hitler, the Nazis had a symbol no opposition party could match.
The hooked cross appeared to many to possess some mystic power of its own.

Hitler might be considered to have been history's most effective demagogue.

The wearing of the uniform of the Hitler Youth had a great advantage. For example, no such member could be given corporal punishment.

*Sieg Heil* means Hail Victory. *Heil Hitler* was designated as the official German greeting. Reich means Empire.

Aides often appeared at rallies with baskets of rose petals for the crowd to strew in Hitler's path. It was forbidden to throw a bouquet his way because "it might contain a bomb."

Two men associated with Hitler made themselves and the dictator very rich men: Max Amann, publisher of *Mein Kampf,* and Heinrich Hofffman, official photographer.

Hitler's speeches often referred to the need to smash Communists and Jews, the need to avenge the Treaty of Versailles, and the need to make Germany victorious over its enemies. Those speeches appealed to emotions rather than intelligence. He was a master of mass emotion.

Hitler's propaganda consisted of conscious and deliberate lies.

Geli Raubal, daughter of Hitler's half-sister, was loved by Hitler. On September 18, 1931 she was found dead in Hitler's Munich home. The coroner's verdict: suicide.

Eva Braun, twenty years younger than Hitler, had few intellectual gifts and had no understanding of politics. She was an excellent swimmer and skier. The empty-headed but attractive blond married Hitler in his last days after being his mistress for twelve years.

A young Eva Braun.

Hitler and his cronies knew they were breaking the law. For them, might was right.

Though nothing was inevitable, Germany proved to be a very fertile ground for Hitler's hatred.

Hitler approved of the Nazi strong-arm tactics and the plans for a network of concentration camps.

Hitler was appointed Chancellor by President Hindenburg. He was not elected. *Jan. 30, 1933*

On July 13, 1933 the Hitler salute became compulsory during the singing of the national anthem. It also became the greeting for all public employees.

Adolf Hitler perceived the disunity among the Allies with uncanny genius.

By 1938, Hitler, who acknowledged no master, had rule over his nation rarely, if ever, equaled in any modern and industrial state.

Disunity among his opponents accounts for some of Hitler's success. Luck was another factor.

The theme of Hitler's Nazism was domination.

Hitler's sense of timing, his gift of simplification, his quickness to accept risks, his genius in politics helped him, an opportunist without principles, to gain and keep control.

Hitler was no fool. The calculation in his actions would never have been possible had he not possessed considerable intellectual powers.

Hitler combined a technical virtuosity with the coarseness and ignorance of a moral illiterate.

According to Hitler, he was selected by Providence to lead; therefore, he believed he was exempt from the usual rules of human conduct.

Hitler tried not to confuse his people by offering them too many enemies for them to hate. He concentrated upon one adversary, and then focused people's hatred upon that "enemy."

We know more about Adolf Hitler than any other dictator in history. Without doubt Hitler was a genius, an evil one, who acknowledged no master. Consistently he showed a distrust of criticism and argument.

Hitler possessed an astonishing power of will. He was an opportunist without principle.

Hitler believed that universal suffrage was "pernicious and destructive" and that democracy was deceitful, i.e., in that all men are created equal.

Hitler believed in his own legend as the invincible conqueror.

Most Germans welcomed Hitler when he came to power in 1933.

The 1933 "Law for the Prevention of Offspring with Hereditary Defects" required that people who were blind, deaf, physically or mentally handicapped, or were alcoholics be sterilized. By 1939 nearly 400 000 people lost their ability to have children.

Hitler surrounded himself and his power with men whose devotion to him was unconditional: Rosenberg, Himmler, Schirach, Hess, Goering, Goebbels, and Streicher, among others.

If an extremist group such as the Nazis were to gain power and mass support, a catastrophe of some sorts would have to take place. The 1929 crisis and the crash of the New York Stock Exchange provided the catastrophe. The depression had a radical effect on the German population.

What passed for ideology was little more than a ragbag of widely felt prejudices, rancour and spite that was full of staggering contradictions, boorish clichés, and empty-headed bigorty. In short it was a set of mutually reinforcing prejudices, but for all its intellectual poverty National Socialism offered an idealistic version of a new society that had a wide appeal. -Kitchen

By late 1932 some type of military regime was likely necessary to replace the Nazi thrust to power.

Hitler and the top Nazis had a relatively easy time with the universities. Professors could be dismissed with the April 7, 1933 Nazi Law if they were deemed unreliable state employees. Many professors, including Jewish individuals, were thusly dismissed. Best known was Albert Einstein.

One wonders why so few of the educated classes recognized the rising Hitler as the embodiment of evil.

The fact that Hitler was underestimated by his rivals was a positive advantage to him.

Hitler believed that all of nature is a great struggle between weakness and strength. There will be an eternal victory of the strong over the weak.

Hitler never received more than approximately 37% of the votes cast in an election.

Hitler wore a cloak of constitutionality, and he turned the law inside out by making illegality legal.

People called Hitler an irrational fanatic, a demoniac individual. He was also a consummately able politician.

Jews were forced to wear two yellow triangles arranged into a Jewish star. Jehovah's Witnesses (many were murdered by the Nazis) wore purple triangles. Homosexuals wore a pink triangle. The 1871 Prussian Penal Code made homosexuality a criminal offense punishable by imprisonment, and still existed when Hitler came to power.

*Until 1746, the law permitted the death penalty for homosexuality in Germany.*

Nearly 3000 priests and pastors from nineteen different occupied countries were sent to the Dachau death camp.

Hitler made no contribution whatever to the spiritual and moral advancement of human beings.

The Nazis under Hitler developed their own marriage, baptism service, and liturgy.

The Third Reich left nothing behind it but horror. The horror of tens of millions dead, of a continent laid to waste, the horror of a great nation reduced to barbarism, moral squalor and mass murder, soon to be crippled by guilt. It is a horror that will not go away, that refuses to distance itself by becoming history; it is the horror of the unfathomable.

Hitler failed to escape in 1945. Since then he has managed to escape complete explanation. In other words, what made Hitler Hitler?: A tough question.

Hitler's life story and career repels and fascinates.

# Sequence of Events

*1889, April 20*: Hitler was born in Braunau, a small town in Upper Austria, across the River Inn from Bavaria, Germany. In the baptismal registry he was entered as Adolfus Hitler. The boy loved his indulgent, kind mother, but likely hated his often drunk, authoritarian, and cruel father, Alois. Adolf was the product of Alois' third marriage, to his second cousin Karla Poelzel, twenty three years his junior.

*1892*: Hitler family moves to Passau, Germany.

*1895*: Hitler family moves to Hafeld near Linz - Hitler begins school, walking to and from Fischlhelm – Adolf Hitler is a good student.

*1897*: Hitler family moves to Lambach a town in between Linz and Salzburg - Hitler attends a school attached to a Benedictine monastery - Hitler is a good student and contemplates a church life.

*1898*: Hitler family move to the outskirts of Linz - Adolf attends Elementary (Volksschule) and is a good student.

*1898*: Edmund Hitler, Adolf's brother, dies of measles at age six – profound change in Adolf from good humored and outgoing to morose and nervous – never again a good student.

*1900, September*: Hitler enters Realschule in Linz, travelling to and from Leonding. Hitler encounters difficulty in school, loses interest, and finds his teachers uninterested in him. His father becomes more upset with him. Hitler wants to become an artist, and father refuses to accept Adolf's wishes.

During this period, Adolf becomes obsessed by the writing of Karl May and the "Redskins". This author was to have a lasting affect on his ideas of geography.

*1901*: Hitler enrolled in another school in Steyr which had lower standards. By age fifteen, Adolf had attended five different secondary schools.

*1903, Jan. 3*: Alois Hitler dies. Adolf becomes male head of the family.

*1904*: Hitler expelled from Realschule in Linz and enters Realschule in Stetr. He is considered a nuisance and lacks the ability to advance to a higher level of education. Following final examinations, Adolf gets drunk and loses his school certificate. He is humiliated at having to ask for another certificate, and vows never to get drunk again, a promise that he apparently keeps for the rest of his life.

*1905*: Adolf fails art school. For two years he wanders about the countryside near Spital, Austria.

*1905*: Adolf's life style now established, study and reading at night, sleeping late in the morning, some light activity in the afternoon and entertainment in the evening.

*1905, Autumn*: Hitler meets August Kubizek who is fascinated by him.

*1906*: Adolf makes his first visit to Vienna. He persuades his mother, now ailing with cancer, to let him move to the Austrian capital.

*1906*: Hitler "falls in love" with a young women named Stephanie; he never meets her, but she later reports that she received a letter from a person saying that he was going to enter the Academy of Art in Vienna and upon completion of his schooling would marry her.

*1906*: Hitler attends Wagner's opera *Rienzi* in Linz; he is deeply moved by the opera, and on a trance-like walk through the city and climb to the top of the Frienberg, he tells Kubizek about his future and how he would become the leader of the people.

*1907, October*: Hitler takes entrance exam at Fine Art Academy in Vienna and is rejected.

*1907, Dec. 21*: Klara Hitler dies, Hitler is grief-stricken.

*1908, February*: Hitler comes to live in Vienna permanently. During this year, he joins the Anti-Semitic League.

*1908, October*: Hitler again fails to get into Fine Arts Academy of Vienna.

*1909:* The year of wandering in Vienna, Hitler starts becoming destitute and apathetic; he ends up living in a shelter for homeless people, and meets Reinhold Hanisn, who helps him survive these hard times.

*1910*: Hitler shows interest in politics.

*1910 – 1913*: Hitler lives at the Mannerheim (home for men) subsists by selling hand-painted post cards.

*1913*: Hitler leaves Vienna. He has no home, trade, profession, and few friends at age twenty-four.

In Munich, Germany he continues his vagabond existence. There he paints and designs posters for businesses and shopkeepers.

*1913*: At age twenty-four, Adolf Hitler is a haggard, sickly loner with no time for women. He begins his "speeches" to those who would listen to his ideas. He stresses his contempt for "that mummy state," Austria.

*1913*: Austrian military authorities list Hitler as a deserter. On February 5, 1914 Austrian army doctors find him too weak and unfit to bear arms.

*1914, January*: Hitler is summoned for military service at Linz. He pleads his case with Austrian authorities and is pronounced innocent.

*1914, June 28*: Princep, a nineteen-year-old member of a Secret Serbian Society, shoots and kills the Archduke Francis Ferdinand and his wife, heir to the Hapsburg throne of the Austrian Hungarian empire. The "shot that was heard around the world" leads to the outbreak of World War I. The Sarajevo murder changes the world.

*1914*: The day Germany declares war, Adolf Hitler is part of the crowd that cheers the declaration in the Odeonplatz in front of the ornate Feldherrn Halle in Munich. A "channa" photograph (one of the most famous photos of that century captures Hitler's happy face and wild eyes. (He later wrote that "the year 1914 was not forced on the masses, but desired by the whole people.")

*1914, August 16:* Hitler joins army - enlists in 16th Bavarian Reserve Infantry - He is a dispatch runner.

*1914:* In early November Hitler is at the front and immediately sees action. German forces, including Hitler are stopped at the first Battle of Ypres. Of 3500 men, 2900 are cut down in four days of fighting.

*1914, December:* Hitler receives Iron Cross.

*1916:* At the fierce Battle of the Somme ,Hitler is hit in one leg by shrapnel and is sent to a hospital in Germany.

*1914 - 1918:* Hitler remains a loner in the army. However, in war he finds his "home". He receives few gifts or letters from friends and relatives during the war.

*1917:* Hitler participates in the Battle of Arras and the third Battle of Ypres.

*1918, July*: Hitler receives Iron Cross 1st Class Medal.

*1918, October*: The British gas attack near Werwick south of Ypres leaves Hitler temporarily blinded.

*1918, October 14*: Hitler temporarily blinded, travels by train to a military hospital at Pasewalk.

*1918, November 10*: A visiting clergyman at the hospital tells the news that Germany had lost the war. The next day an armistice is signed at Compiegne in France.

*Hitler later said that then he broke down and wept - the first time since his mother's death.*

*1918, November 11*: War ends.

*1919, September*: Hitler examines and visits a small political group in Munich called the German Workers' Party.

*1919, September*: Hitler, while working for the army, prepares a document on the proper attitude to be cultivated toward Jews. It is his first political document.

*1920*: General Ludendorff meets with Hitler and Eckert.

*1921*: The "nameless" joiner, Hitler, makes himself dictator of the party.

*Subordinate leaders included army officer Ernst Roehm, famous war pilot and drug addict Hermann Goering, drunken and deranged poet Dietrich Eckart, student Rudolf Hess, Alfred Rosenberg, druggist Gregor Strassor, teacher Julius Streicher, Joseph Goebbles, and chicken farmer Heinrich Himmler.*

*1921*: By summer, Hitler takes over undisputed leadership of the Nazi Party. Der Führer has emerged.

*1922*: Hitler is locally known as "King of Munich".

*1922*: Adolf Hitler surrounds himself with a diverse group from every class which embraces a wide spectrum of cultures and occupations. All share his nationalism and fear of Marxism.

*1923, September 25*: At a meeting of the heads of all right wing military formations and private armies he convinces them that they will be more effective under his overall command.

*1923, November 8*: In Munich, Hitler makes his bid for dictatorship of Germany. Firing his pistol at the ceiling after jumping on a table Hitler shouts: "The national revolution has begun."

*1923, November 9*: With a ragged column of storm troopers, Hitler, Goering, and Ludendorff march to the center of Munich, where they are met by police Within seconds, sixteen Nazis and three policemen are dead. Goering is wounded. Hitler escapes in a waiting car. His shoulder is dislocated in the incident: a flop indeed.

*1924*: Hitler is found guilty of high treason and is sentenced to five years imprisonment at Landsberg.

*1924*: Resumes work on Mein Kampf.

*1924*: Hitler returns to his Munich home just before Christmas – freed from Landsberg.

*1924 – 1929*: The Nazi Party and its press are banned. Economic revival comes to Germany and Hitler's party loses much of its appeal. He claims correctly that it will take five years to restrengthen his movement. Good times in Germany means bad times for the Nazis.

*1925, February 26*: Over 4000 followers hear Hitler's two-hour harangue at the very site of the failed 1923 putsch.

*1925, February 27*: Hitler gives his first speech since his release from prison to a crowd of about 2000. Shortly thereafter, the Bavarian Government revokes his license to speak, fearing that he would cause trouble.

*1925, March*: The Nazis special presidental election receives only 211 000 votes out of a total of almost twenty-seven million. A second election follows with Field Marshal von Hindenburg winning a narrow victory.

*1925*: By the end of the year, 27 000 dues-paying party members are attracted. Four years later that number increases by 40%. In 1928, the Nazis poll fewer than one million votes out of the thirty-one million cast, and they elect only twelve of the Reichstag's 491 members.

*1925*: Hitler renounces his Austrian citizenship.

*1925 - 1929*: Hitler creates the Hitler Youth, patterned after Mussolini's *Avanguardisti*, for German children age 15 to 18. Younger children are also organized into groups. He divides the country into districts called *Gau*, one for each of the nation's thirty-four electoral districts.

*1925 - 1929*: The Nazi membership increases from 27 000 in 1925 to 178 000 in 1929.

*1928*: Hitler's half-sister, Angela Raubal, comes from Vienna to keep house for him. Her two daughters also come. Hitler, age 39, falls in love with the elder, winsome daughter, Geli, age 20.

*1929*: Hitler chooses the mild-mannered chicken farmer Heinrich Himmler to command the SS.

*1929, October 24:* The Wall Street stock market crashes. Perhaps no European country suffers more than Germany during the resultant depression. Millions despair.

*1930:* Until 1930, the Nazis are a minor group on the fringe of German politics.

*1930, October:* Offers Ernst Roehm a post as head of the S.A.

*1931, January 1:* Former Barlow Palace in Munich, now renamed the Brown House, opens as headquarters of the National Socialist Party.

*1931, September 18:* Hitler's niece, Geli Raubel, with whom he was in love, commits suicide in Munich at age 23.

*1932:* Hitler runs for president against the eighty-four-year-old Field Marshall Paul von Hindenburg, who is elected with a 53% majority. Hitler receives 37%.

*1933, January 4:* Hitler, Papen, and Baron Vonschroesour hold a secret meeting to decide future of Germany. Papen sees joint rule, Hitler has no intention of sharing power.

*1933, January. 30*: Just before noon, Adolf Hitler, the one-time Vienna tramp and self-styled revolutionary, becomes Chancellor of the German Republic he had sworn to destroy. It takes him a year and one half to become absolute dictator of Germany.

*1933, February 27*: The Reichstag burns; Nazis use the occasion as pretext to arrest one thousand Communists: a propaganda victory.

*1933, April 7*: The Nazi law decrees the dismissal of all Jews from government service and universities, and bars them from the sciences, medicine, law, and engineering.

*1933, May 20*: Books unacceptable to Nazi Party are burned on the Unter Den Linden opposite Berlin University. These include authors such as Einstein, Thomas Mann, Erich Maria Remarque, H. G. Wells, and many others.

*1933*: Unions are dissolved, other political parties are banned on July 14, 1933.

*1933, July 20*: Hitler concludes the Concordat (Treaty) with the Vatican, which is to guarantee freedom of religion for Catholics. It doesn't happen.

*1933*: Nazi Party Day in Nuremberg. Ernst Roehm stands in place of Honor next to Hitler.

*1934, June 25:* Roehm and other "enemies" of Hitler are arrested.

*1934, June 30*: Hitler gives signal for massacre known as Night of the Long Knives to begin.

*1934, August 2*: President Hinderberg dies. Hitler abolishes title of President and proclaims himself Führer and Reich Chancellor.

*1934, August 2*: Armed forces are made to swear undying loyalty and unconditional obedience to Hitler.

*1934, August 19*: A plebiscite is held to determine if the people want Hitler to remain as head of state. As there is no other candidate, Hitler wins, and is able to say that he is head of state by direct will of the people.

*1935, Spring*: Rearmament and universal military service are introduced. Hitler announces the introduction of military conscription, and determines the German army's strength at thirty-six divisions, roughly 550 000 men.

*The Reichstag cheered when Hitler announced that he takes full responsibility for the purge.*

*1935, November 2*: Jews are debarred from owning any property, and they cannot work as artisans. Over 200 000 Jews manage to leave the country during the period.

*1936, Spring*: German troops march into the Rhineland. Not a shot is fired. Hitler states there will be no more territorial claims in Europe.

*1936, June*: Olympic Games are held in Berlin.

*1936, December 1*: the entire German youth within the borders of the Reich is organized in the Hitler Youth.

*1937*: The so-called Hossbach Memorandum is formulated, which stresses the need for Germany to acquire *lebensraum* or living space.

*1938, February*:  Hitler meets with Chancellor Von Schuschnige of Austria and coerces him into signing a document joining Austria in economic union with Germany, giving amnesty to all National Socialist prisoners, and giving the offices of Ministry of Interior, Ministry of War, and Ministry of Finance to National Socialists: the Anschluss.

*1938, March 14*: Hitler enters Vienna as conqueror of a city he has always disliked.

*1938, May*: Hitler begins to prepare for takeover of the Sudetenland.

*1938, September*: Agreement between Germany, the U.K., France, and Italy regarding the Sudetenland is signed: the "Munich Agreement." Chamberlain returns to London proclaiming "Peace in our time."

*1938, November 7*: Herschel Grynszpan, a Polish Jew, shoots Ernst Von Rath in German embassy in Paris. Von Rath dies two days later. This event precipitates an orgy of burning, looting, and killing in Germany, known as *Krystallnacht*.

*1938*: Jewish women in Germany are compelled by law to adopt the middle name of Sari, and all Jewish men that of Israel.

*1939, March 15:* Germany invades Czechoslovakia. Czechoslovakia ceases to exist and is now the Protectorate of Bohemia and Moravia.

*1939, April 14*: President Roosevelt appeals to Hitler and Mussolini to safeguard peace by promising a guaranteed period of nonaggression.

*1939, May 22*: Hitler and Mussolini form the Pact of Steel.

*1939, August 23*: The Russo-German pact is signed leading to the two powers taking over Poland.

*1939, September 1*: Germany invades Poland. The result is war.

# Appendix A

## Program of the National Socialist German Workers' Party

The Program of the German Workers' Party is a limited program. Its leaders have no intention, once its aims have been achieved, of establishing new ones, merely in order to insure the continued existence of the party by the artificial creations of discontent among the masses.

1. We demand, on the basis of the right of national self-determination, the union of all Germans in a Greater Germany.

2. We demand equality for the German nation among other nations, and the revocation of the peace treaties of Versailles and Saint-Germain.

3. We demand land (colonies) to feed our people and to settle our excess population.

4. Only a racial comrade can be a citizen. Only a person of German blood, irrespective of religious denomination, can be a racial comrade. No Jew, therefore, can be a racial comrade.

5. Noncitizens shall be able to live in Germany as guests only, and must be placed under alien legislation.

6. We therefore demand that every public office, no matter of what kind, and no matter whether it be national, state, or local office, be held by none but citizens.

7. We demand that the state make it its primary duty to provide a livelihood for its citizens. If it should prove impossible to feed the entire population, the members of foreign nations (non-citizens) are to be expelled from Germany.

8. Any further immigration of non-Germans is to be prevented. We demand that all non-Germans who entered Germany after August 2, 1914, be forced to leave the Reich without delay.

9. All citizens are to possess equal rights and obligations.

10. It must be the first duty of every citizen to perform mental or physical work. Individual activity must not violate the general interest, but must be exercised within the framework of the community, and for the general good.

THEREFORE WE DEMAND:

11. The abolition of all income unearned by work and trouble.

# BREAK THE SLAVERY OF INTEREST

12. In view of the tremendous sacrifices of life and property imposed by any war on the nation, personal gain from the war must be characterized as a crime against the nation. We therefore demand the total confiscation of all war profits.

13. We demand the nationalization of all business enterprises that have been organized into corporations (trusts).

14. We demand profit-sharing in large industrial enterprises.

15. We demand the generous development of old age insurance.

16. We demand the creation and support of a healthy middle class, and the immediate socialization of the huge department stores and their lease, at low rates, to small tradesmen. We demand that as far as national, state, or municipal purchases are concerned, the utmost consideration be shown to small tradesmen.

17. We demand a land reform suitable to our national needs, and the creation of a law for the expropriation without compensation of land for communal purposes. We demand the abolition of ground rent, and the prohibition of all speculation in land.

18. We demand a ruthless battle against those who, by their activities, injure the general good. Common criminals, usurers, profiteers, etc., are to be punished by death, regardless of faith or race.

19. We demand that Roman law, which serves a materialist world order, be replaced by German law.

20. To open the doors of higher education – and thus to leading positions – to every able and hard-working German, the state must provide for a thorough restructuring of our entire educational system. The curricula of all educational institutions are to be brought into line with the requirements of practical life. As soon as the mind begins to develop, the schools must teach civic thought (citizenship classes). We demand the education, at state expense, of particularly talented children of poor parents, regardless of the latters' class or occupation.

21. The state must see to it that national health standards are raised. It must do so by protecting mothers and children, by prohibiting child labor, by promoting physical strength through legislation providing for compulsory gymnastics and sports, and by the greatest possible support for all organizations engaged in the physical training of youth.

22. We demand the abolition of the mercenary army and the creation of a people's army.

23. We demand legal warfare against intentional political lies and their dissemination through the press. To facilitate the creation of a German press, we demand:

a. that all editors of, and contributors to, newspapers that appear in the German language be racial comrades;

b. that no non-German newspaper may appear without the express permission of the government. Such papers may not be printed in the German language;

c. that non-Germans shall be forbidden by law to hold any financial share in a German newspaper, or to influence it in any way.

We demand that the penalty for violating such a law shall be the closing of the newspapers involved, and the immediate expulsion of the non-Germans involved.

Newspapers which violate the general good are to be banned. We demand legal warfare against those tendencies in art and literature which exert an undermining influence on our national life, and the suppression of cultural events which violate this demand.

24. We demand freedom for all religious denominations, provided they do not endanger the existence of the state,

or violate the moral and ethical feelings of the Germanic race. The party, as such, stands for positive Christianity, without, however, allying itself to any particular denomination. It combats the Jewish-materialistic spirit within and around us, and is convinced that a permanent recovery of our people can be achieved only from within, on the basis of

## THE COMMON INTEREST BEFORE SELF-INTEREST

25. To implement all these points, we demand the creation of a strong central power in Germany. A central political parliament should possess unconditional authority over the entire Reich, and its organization in general.

Corporations based on estate and profession should be formed to apply the general legislation passed by that Reich in the various German states.

The leaders of the party promise to do everything that is in their power, and if need be, to risk their very lives, to translate this program into action.

Munich, February 24, 1920.

Gottfried Feder, *Das programm der N.S.D.A.P und seine seltanschaulichen Grundgedanken* (Munich, 1932), pp. 19-22.

# Appendix B

## Average Annual Unemployment Figures in Germany, 1932-1938

| Year | Number of Unemployed |
|------|----------------------|
| 1932 | 5 575 500 |
| 1933 | 4 004 400 |
| 1934 | 2 718 300 |
| 1935 | 2 151 000 |
| 1936 | 1 592 700 |
| 1937 | 912 300 |
| 1938 | 429 500 |

*Der Große Brockhauss (Weisbaden, 1952), I, 374.*

## Unemployment in Germany, in percentiles of the Labour Force

| | |
|------|------|
| 1932 | 30.1 |
| 1938 | 2.1 |

*Der Große Herder (Freiburg, 1952), I, 374.*

# Appendix C

## Unemployment in Germany, 1924-1932

| 1924 | 1928 | 1930 | Jul. 31, 1932 | Oct. 31, 1932 |
|---|---|---|---|---|
| 978 000 | 1 368 000 | 3 076 000 | 5 392 000 | 5 109 000 |

The figures are those of annual average unemployment, except for 1932, where some precise end-of-the-month figures are available, and the two dates that coincide with the Reichstag elections are given. The election statistics are from Harry Pross, *Die Zerstorung der deutschen Politik* (Frankfurt, 1959), p. 352; those on unemployment from Saitzow, *Die Aarbeitslosigkeit*, p. 148-49, and *Statisches Jahrbuch*, 1933, p. 19.

# Appendix D

## Bankruptcies in Germany, 1928-1932

| Year | Number of Bankruptcies |
|------|------------------------|
| 1928 | 10 595 |
| 1929 | 13 180 |
| 1930 | 15 486 |
| 1931 | 19 254 |
| 1932 | 14 138 |

*Statistiches Jahrbuch*, 1929, p. 354; 1930. p. 398; 1931, p. 378; 1932, p. 374; 1933. p. 384.

# Appendix E

## Losses in the German army and navy

calculated on the basis of the official casualty lists up to no. 1,284 of October 24, 1918 were:

|       | Killed    | Wounded   | Missing | Total     |
|-------|-----------|-----------|---------|-----------|
| Army  | 1 582 244 | 3 654 175 | 756 843 | 5 993 262 |
| Navy  | 28 860    | 28 968    | 15 679  | 73 507    |
| Total | 1 611 104 | 3 683 143 | 772 522 | 6 066 769 |

A large proportion of the missing, certainly nine-tenths, must be reckoned as dead, so that the total number of deaths, according to this statement, must be put at about 2 300 000.

Samuel Duman and dK. O. Vedel-Peterson,
*Losses of Life Caused by War* (Oxford, 1923) p. 141.

# Appendix F

## Elections to the Reichstag, 1924-1932

|  | May 4, 1924 | Dec 7, 1924 |
|---|---|---|
| Number of Eligible Voters (millions) | 38.4 | 39.0 |
| Votes Cast (millions) | 29.7 | 30.7 |
| National Socialist German Workers Party | 1 918 000 6.6% | 908 000 3% |
| German Nationalist People's Party (Conservative) | 5 696 000 19.5% | 6 209 000 20.5% |
| Center Party (Catholic) | 3 914 000 13.4% | 4 121 000 13.6% |
| Democratic Party (German State Party) | 1 655 000 5.7% | 1 921 000 6.3% |
| Social Democratic Party | 6 009 000 20.5% | 7 886 000 26% |
| Communist Party | 3 693 000 12.6% | 2 712 000 9% |

|  | May 20, 1928 | Sep 14, 1930 | Jul 31, 1932 | Nov 6 1932 |
|---|---|---|---|---|
|  | 41.2 | 43.0 | 44.2 | 44.2 |
|  | 31.2 | 35.2 | 37.2 | 35.7 |
|  | 810 000<br>2.6% | 6 407 000<br>18.3% | 13 779 000<br>37.3% | 11 737 000<br>33.1% |
|  | 4 382 000<br>14.2% | 2 458 000<br>7% | 2 187 000<br>5.9% | 3 131 000<br>8.8% |
|  | 3 712 000<br>12.1% | 4 127 000<br>11.8% | 4 589 000<br>12.4% | 4 230 000<br>11.9% |
|  | 1 506 000<br>4.9% | 1 322 000<br>3.8% | 373 000<br>1% | 339 000<br>1% |
|  | 9 153 000<br>29.8% | 8 576 000<br>24.5% | 7 960 000<br>21.6% | 7 251 000<br>20.4% |
|  | 3 265 000<br>10.6% | 4 590 000<br>13.1% | 5 370 000<br>14.3% | 5 980 000<br>16.9% |

# Appendix G

## Law Concerning the Hitler Youth of December 1, 1936

It is on youth that the future of the German nation depends. Hence, it is necessary to prepare the entire German youth for its coming duties.

The government therefore has passed the following law, which is being proclaimed herewith:

### ARTICLE 1

The entire German youth within the borders of the Reich is organized in the Hitler Youth.

### ARTICLE 2

It is not only in home and school, but in the Hitler Youth as well that all of Germany's youth is to be educated, physically, mentally, and morally, in the spirit of National Socialism, to serve the nation and the racial community.

## ARTICLE 3

The task of educating the entire German youth is entrusted to the Reich Youth Leader of the National Socialist German Workers' Party. He thus becomes the "Youth Leader of the German Reich." His office shall rank with that of a ministry. He shall reside in Berlin, and be responsible directly to the Führer and Chancellor.

## ARTICLE 4

The administrative instructions and legal regulations necessary to implement and supplement this law shall be issued by the Führer and Chancellor.

Berlin, December 1, 1936
The Führer and Chancellor
s. ADOLF HITLER

Jacobsen and Jochmann, *Ausgewahlte Dopkumente*, I, n.p.

# Bibliography

Alexander, Bevin, *How Hitler Could Have Won World War II*. New York, Crown Publishers, 2000

Bard, Mitchell G. (Ed.), *The Holocaust*. San Diego, Greenhaven Press, 2001

Bartoletti, Susan Campbell, *Hitler Youth: Growing Up in Hitler's Shadow*. New York, Scholastic Inc., 2005

Berthon, Simon and Potts, Joanna. *Warlords*. Cambridge, Da Capo Press, 2006

Bessel, Richard. *Nazism And War*. London, Phoenix Paperback, 2004

Black, Edwin. *IBM and the Holocaust*. New York, Crown Publishers, 2001

Blond, Georges. *The Death of Hitler's Germany*. New York, Pyramid Books, 1948

Bullock, Allan. *Hitler: a Study in Tyranny*. New York, Bantam Books, 1958

Bullock, Allan. *Hitler and Stalin: Parallel Lives*. London, Fontana Press, 1998

Carroll, James. *Constantine's Sword: the Church And the Jews.* Boston, Houghton Mifflin Co., 2001.

Churchill, Winston S. "Adolf Hitler" *Memoirs of the Second World War.* Boston, Houghton Mifflin Co., 1959

Collins, James L. (Ed.). *The Marshall Cavendish Illustrated Encyclopedia of World War II.* Vol. I, 1966.

Cook, Ramsay et al, *Canada, a Modern Study.* Toronto, Clark Irwin & Co. 1963

Crew, David F. *Hitler and the Nazis: A History in Documents.* New York, Oxford University Press, 2005

Damon, Duane. *Mein Kampf.* London, Thomson/Gale, 2003

Darmon, Peter (Ed.) *The Third Reich Day By Day.* The Grange, The Brown Reference Group, 2004

Engelmann, Bernt. *Hitler's Germany.* New York, Pantheon Books, 1986

Evans, Richard J. *The Coming Of The Third Reich.* New York, The Penguin Press, 2004

Evans, Richard J. *The Third Reich In Power.* New York, Penguin Press, 2005

Fest, Joachim C. *Hitler.* New York, Harcourt Brace Jovanovich, 1973 (Translated Version).

Fiorni, Flavio (Ed.) *A New Illustrated History of the Nazis.* Milan, A David & Charles Book, 2005

Flood, Charles B. *Hitler, the Path to Power.* New York, Houghton Mifflin. 1989

Friedlander, Saul. *The Years of Extermination.* New York, Harper Collins, 2007

Friedman, Ina R. *The Other Victims: First Person Stories of Non-Jews Persecuted by the Nazis.* New York, Houghton Mifflin, 1990.

Fuchs, Thomas. *The Hitler Fact Book.* Los Angeles, Fountain Books, 1990.

Gabori, George. *When Evils Were Most Free.* Toronto, McClelland and Stewart - Bantam Ltd., 1982

Gervais, Frank. *Adolph Hitler.* New York, Hawthorne Books, 1974

Halleck, Elaine (Ed.) *Living in Nazi Germany*. London, Thomson/Gale, 2004

Harclerode, Peter and Pittaway, Brendan. *The Last Masters: World War II and the Looting of Europe's Treasure Houses*. New York, Welcome Rain Publishers, 1999

Harries, Meiron and Susie. *The Last Days of Innocence*. New York, Random House, 1998

Hitler, Adolf. *Mein Kampf*. Boston, Houghton Mifflin Co., 1943

Hoffman, Sebastian. *Failure of a Revolution*. (Translated) London, Andre Dursch, 1973, p. 103

Hutchinson, Bruce. *The Incredible Canadian*. Toronto, Longmans Green & Co. 1969

Hutchinson, Bruce. *The Unknown Country*. Toronto, Longmans Green & Co. 1948

Kater, Michael H. *Hitler Youth*. London, Harvard University Press 2004

Keely, Jennifer. *Life In the Hitler Youth*. San Diego, Lucent Books, 2000

Kershaw, Ian. *Hitler: 1889-1936. Hubris.* New York, W.W. Norton. 1999

Kershaw, Ian. *Hitler 1936-1945: Nemesis.* London, W. W. Norton & Co., 2000

Kitchen, Martin. *The Third Reich.* Gloucestershire, Tempus, 2007.

Kjelle, Marylou M. *Hitler and His Henchmen.* London, Thornson/Gale, 2005

Koch, H.W. *Hitler Youth: The Duped Generation.* New York, Ballantine Books, 1972

Koonz, Claudia. *Mothers in the Fatherland: Women, the Family, and Nazi Politics.* New York, St. Martin's, 1987

Langer, Walter C. *The Mind of Adolph Hitler.* New York, Basic Books, 1973

Lattimer, John K. *Hitler and the Nazi Leaders: A Unique Insight Into Evil.* New York, Hippocrene Books, Inc., 2001

Lewen, Ronald. *Hitler's Mistakes.* New York, William Morrow & Co. Inc. 1984

Lioddeell Hart B.H. *History of the Second World War.* New York, G.P. Putnam's Sons. 1970

Lokacs, John. *The Hitler of History.* New York, Vintage Books, 1997

Lower, A.R.M. *Colony to Nation: A History of Canada.* Don Mills, Longmans Canada Ltd. 1964

Mantanle, Ivor. *Adolph Hitler: A Photographic Documentary.* London, Crescent Books, 1983

Mitcham Jr., Samuel W. *Why Hitler? The Genesis of the Nazi Reich.* Westport, Praiger Publishers, 1996

Overy, Richard. *The Dictators: Hitler's Germany, Stalin's Russia,* London, W.W. Norton and Co., 2004

Payne, Robert. *The Life and Death of Adolf Hitler.* New York, Praiger Publishers, 1973

Payne, Stanley G. *Franco and Hitler.* Yale, Yale University Press, 2008

Princle, Heather. *The Master Plan: Himmler's Scholars and the Holocaust.* New York, Hyperion, 2006

Remak, Joachim. *The Nazi Years: A Documentary.* Englewood Cliffs, Prentice-Hall Inc., 1969

Roberts, Andrew. *Hitler and Churchill.* London, Phoenix Publishers, 2003

Roeloff, Tamara L. (Ed.) *The Holocaust: Death Camps.* San Diego, Greenhaven Press, 2002

Rosenbaum, Ron. *Explaining Hitler: The Search for the Origins of His Evil.* New York, Random House, 1998

Roth, Joseph. *What I Saw: Reports from Berlin 1920-1933,* London, W.W. Norton & Co., 1996

Schramm, Percy Ernst. *Hitler: The Man and the Military Leader.* Chicago: Quadrangle Books, 1971

Schwarzwaller, Wolf. *The Unknown Hitler: His Private Life And Fortune.* New York, Stoddart Publisher, N.D.

Shirer, William L. *Berlin Diary.* New York, Alfred A. Knopf, 1941

Shirer, William L. *The Rise and Fall of Adolph Hitler.* New York, Scholastic Book Services, 1961

Speer, Albert. *Inside the Third Reich.* New York, Galahad Books, 1970

Stalcup, Brenda (Ed.) *Adolf Hitler*. San Diego, Greenhaven Publ. 2000

Stone, Norman. *Hitler*. Toronto, Little, Brown and Co., 1980.

Toland, John. *Adolph Hitler*. New York, Ballantine Books, 1976

Van Der Vat, Dan. *The Good Nazi: The Life and Lies of Albert Speer*. New York, Houghton Mifflin Co., 1977

Von Lang, Jochen. *Top Nazi*. New York, Enigma Books, 2005

Waite, Robert G. L. (Ed.) *Hitler And Nazi Germany*. Toronto, Holt Rinehart and Winston, 1965.

Willows, Donald C. and Richmond Stewart. *Canada: Colony to Centenniel*, Toronto, McGraw Hill Co. 1970

Zapruder, Alexandra (Ed.) *Salvaged Pages*. London, Yale University Press, 2002

Ziegler, Jean. *The Swiss, the Gold, And The Dead: How Swiss Banks Helped Finance the Nazi War Machine*. New York, Harcourt Brace & Co., 1997

**Colin A. Thomson** is a writer, historian, and professor emeritus of the University of Lethbridge. He has served at the University of Alberta and the University of Saskatchewan, as well as Kenya, Leostho, and Nigeria. He is the author of numerous academic papers and books, including *Sounds Like Alberta* with F. Lee Prindle, *Swift Runner*, *The Romance of Alberta Settlements*, *The Romance of Manitoba Settlements*, *Fourteen*, and *Klanty's daughters* (published by Detselig Enterprises), as well as *Blacks in Deep Snow*, *Born with as Call*, *Romance of Saskatchewan Settlements* with Rodney G. Thomson, *The Flavor of Baseball: The First 160 Years* with F. Lee Prindle, and *Snookered*.

**William E. Lingard** is a retired speech language pathologist long active in the Lethbridge Historical Society. He has co-authored *The Butcher, the Baker, the Candy Maker, 1870–1920: A Guide to the First Fifty Years of Commerce in Lethbridge*, and *The History of Business Activities in Lethbridge*.